The
Christian
Year

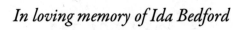

In loving memory of Ida Bedford

The Christian Year

Evelyn Francis Capel

Floris Books

First published by the Christian Community Press,
London in 1967
This edition published 2012

British Library CIP Data available
ISBN 978-086315-897-1
Printed in Great Britain
by TJ International, Cornwall

CONTENTS

PROLOGUE

This is a classic text, so some gender-specific pronouns and references to Man, Mankind, etc have been preserved as they were in Evelyn Capel's original work.

THE SEASONS

The background to the drama of human existence is the changing scenery of the earth's seasons. Winter changes to spring, spring to summer, summer to autumn in much the same way each year. Their magical transformations can be relied upon but the wonder of the magic never grows stale with repetition. Spring has come before, it will come again, but there is a particular note, a subtle effluence, a shade of feeling in this spring that has never been quite the same before and which will haunt the expectation of next spring, though it will not be realised again. A particular season can be lost to one's experience if, in the midst of the pleasure in finding again its well-known, often repeated character, the heart does not catch the inner quality that can only be apprehended this once. It is a joy to find in spring the crocuses coming into blossom under the same tree where they have been growing for years, to catch in the height of summer the familiar scent of new mown hay, to watch in the autumn the blue smoke of a bonfire rising past the bronzed leaves still fast in the branches and to sense in winter the tang of a clear frosty morning. Yet there is, amidst the familiar joys, the thrill of the unrepeatable element that makes each season in its own year an event of a lifetime, if only one is awake enough not to miss it.

When a new season is approaching, the heart begins to ask, what will it be this time, where shall I find it, when will the moment of comprehension come? To everyone who looks, it is shown, however varied the time, place and manner of the showing. When the unrepeatable quality is felt and recognised, we have a glimpse into the lasting reality behind the changing scenery we see around us.

How different is the experience of walking through a landscape in winter and summer. When the trees are in leaf, the grass and the corn high, the flowers in blossom, one's gaze is drawn upwards. The sky is blue and bright with sunshine and across it sail the great white ships of cloud. The vivid colours of the flowers and the fluttering butterflies keep one looking this way and that. The ground is unnoticed beneath its coat of many colours. But in the winter the balance of the landscape is reversed. The sky is covered with dark cloud, or, when it is clear, it is pale and remote. One's eye is now drawn to the dark outlines of the trees, and to the browns, greens and blacks of the bare landscape. The earth's forces now tend strongly downward, while the sky has an air of remoteness. After a snowfall the "downwardness" is intensified. The colour and brightness is below, while the sky above is leaden grey or misty blue. Thus the life of the earth visibly changes with the season. In spring and summer it is poured out into the air and the light in the multitude of leaves, blossoms and fruit. In autumn and winter it enters the earth and underneath the surface is concentrated in activity and preparation for the outpouring of the next spring.

The seasons as they follow each other in the round of the year constitute the earth's way of life. Periods of inner activity when outwardly her surface is still and quiet alternate with periods of great outer activity, when her life is poured out through the growing, moving multitude of her creatures who flourish in summertime. In all this the sun is her partner, bringing about in conjunction with her the changes of the seasons. When he is high in the sky and shines down in his greatest strength, the earth blossoms to the full. When his orb hangs low, his beams are weak and his might least; the earth turns in on herself, leaving her surface bare. Other heavenly bodies also send their influences earthward.

The moon wields the powers of growth. The rhythm of her waxing and waning governs and regulates all growing plants, animals and even children. Whoever is interested in the growing of things in garden or field looks frequently at the moon, for his plants will thrive only if his own efforts harmonise with her rule. Yet though the farmer and the gardener think much about the weather, wanting rain or dry weather, fearing frost and welcoming its toughening effect, praising sunshine and longing for cool breezes, it is strange to observe, as one certainly can, that the plants themselves are less dependent on the changeful weather than those who cultivate them actually expect. Of late years, the weather has surely grown more distressed than it was once, with more unseasonable weather and more capricious changes reflecting the unsettled state of human affairs; nevertheless flowers and crops of all kinds grow and bear fruit. The hidden, powerful influences from the Heavens, from beyond the earth's atmosphere, determine how they grow.

If one stops to examine the plants growing in a few yards of an English hedgerow, leaves of the most varied shapes are found, some tending to be round and a little fleshy, others shaped like lances, still others broad and many-pointed. Just as varied is the manner in which the leaves are set on the stem. Some spread out in rosettes from a centre on the ground. Others appear at intervals from a central, upward-thrusting stem. The leaves may project opposite to each other in pairs, or they may grow each in his own place on the stalk, so that when one looks downward from the top they appear to be spiralling upwards. The varying influences and motions of the stars are reflected in the plant forms. If one would see the effect in relation to cause one should, after watching the wonder of forms and colours in field, wood and hedgerow by daylight, lift in the darkness of night one's eyes to the star-filled sky and contemplate the shining eyes of the beings of God as they radiate forth in their beams the forces with which, out of their divine power of giving, they bless the created world. The world of origins shows its outer appearance in the mysterious pictures traced in light on the background of night blue.

As a practical example let us look at how some of the trees grow in relation to the planets moving overhead. The tree which is most completely under the influence of Saturn is the hornbeam. That which most clearly expresses the character of Jupiter is the maple, whilst Mars declares himself distinctly in the oak. The nature of the Sun is mirrored in the ash tree, of Mercury in the elm, of Venus in the birch. The Moon has put her impress most clearly in the cherry tree. To study the shapes and characters of these trees is to become acquainted with the individual nature of the different planets. Likewise all that may be learnt about the separate character of the planets may illumine the particular style of the trees in which they are reflected. The influence of the planets is at work also in the sphere of metals and minerals. The same cosmic influences inspire their colours and crystalline forms as determine the forms of flowers and plants; and just as the seasons originate from the changing relationship of the earth to the heavenly bodies under the regency of the Sun and the myriad forms of plants and minerals reflect the stars, so do the planets weave their influences together to produce the fabric of the human soul. Before birth each human being is fitted out with a soul garment that he will wear on earth. It is a Joseph's coat of many colours that each one receives from the hands of the beings of God, who look down to us through the eyes of the stars. Everyone, as he goes about the business of living, is aware of certain feelings and tendencies of thought. He knows that to some degree everyone shares the same, but in varying proportions which make up the particular cast of his character. This garment of many colours varies in shade from person to person, but the essential tones are the same. Each planet has sent his own ray of influence to weave in the soul. The tendency to inwardness of heart, to ponder over the meaning of the world and of experience comes into the soul from Saturn. The inner wisdom that can shine from the heart into our experience of the world is the working of Jupiter. The active going forth to meet and experience the world is given by Mars. The faculty of movement, of having experience by moving from one thing or one thought on to the next is sent by Mercury. The grace of heart that beautifies experience and behaviour is the blessing of Venus. The intelligence to grasp experience and enter the world reflects the force of the Moon. The radiating power of heart and will is derived from the Sun.

In the Heavens the planets circle in their courses, maintaining the harmony of the world order. The souls of human beings are woven in this sphere but when they have been released from the heavenly world into the realm of the earth, the powers that work disorder can enter and disturb the divine pattern. Everyone, during the span of their life on earth, has to become their own sun in the world within, where the forces of the planets are reflected, and has to establish out of their own effort tranquillity and harmony. They turn the power of their will inwards upon themselves, that they may rule the kingdom of their soul, as the sun rules the starry realm in the sky.

Outside ourselves in physical form and in the manner of growth and life, we may read of the existence of the stars. When we look within ourselves we find this again in another medium of expression, in the weaving, moving forces of the soul. It is a simple matter of observation to see that our human life is related to that of the earth. Our bodily feelings of well- or ill-being vary with the seasons and the weather. Our habits of living and our moods change likewise. But there is a further more subtle observation, which goes to show that the whole life of our soul moves with the earth's rhythm of the seasons.

This is mysterious but not difficult to comprehend, when once experience has illumined the idea that the planets who manifest themselves in our thinking and feeling do so at the same time in the earth's plants and stones. They are expressing, just as our thoughts and feelings do, a kind of soul life. But whose? That of the earth herself. If other planets are beings, who gaze down through the eyes of the stars and influence the sphere of soul, why not the earth? Her way of life in the seasons is that of being endowed with soul. When she puts forth her flowers in spring and summer, they are her thoughts, not indeed wakeful ones, as ours should be, but dreams set forth in green leaves of many shapes and in coloured blossoms fragrant with her feeling. They have warm joyful scents, and bitter sharp ones, just as we have conditions of joy and of bitterness in our human souls. The earth has her life of soul, but the form it takes is different from that which we know in ourselves, and yet it is closely related. All the community of the earth's creatures, animals, plants and stones share in her life of soul, having their existence within it, manifesting it in their behaviour.

Our human life of soul is clearly interwoven with that of the earth. The outer reaction of people to the changing seasons is clear enough, but an inner rhythm is also present. It can be watched in our awareness of ourselves. In wintertime the soul tends to withdraw into the bodily house, to concentrate inwardly so that the sense of self is strengthened. Her own activity and thinking becomes more alive and conscious. The individual will, not stimulated at this season from outside, consolidates its forces. As the life of Nature sinks away from her perception, the human soul finds her life from within and is intensely aware of independent selfhood.

When the sun's light and warmth increases, the soul begins to expand. The "self-centredness" of the winter turns into the "world-centredness" of the summer. The soul would become one-sided if the winter state would last too long. The cosmic warmth that causes the flowers to blossom, enlivens and warms the soul. This is something different from the sense of well-being which makes most people conscious of greater enjoyment in summer. Beneath such emotions on the surface, the soul is aware of reaching outward and upwards with the scent and colour of the flowers towards the world of her own origin. She goes to meet the beings of the stars and planets from which she was born, and refreshed with their touch will be able to return into herself for the other half of the year. The mood of summer is dreamy compared with the greater wakefulness of winter. The sense of being upheld and enlivened by the universe, of receiving one's being as a cosmic gift, of having been fashioned as a creature of God comes uppermost in the heart. A particular pleasure is to be felt in recognising the kinship of one's human being to that of all the other creatures, of feeling oneself drawn towards the world-warmth in company with flowers, birds and animals. The joy of summer, which has its outer reflection in the holiday mood, comes from perceiving how much blessing and strength is given to the human soul by the world. It takes courage when this season is over to turn inwards again and make the effort to cultivate in one's self the gifts of God that they may bring forth fruit in the inner place of the soul.

The soul life of human beings follows so closely the rhythm of the seasons because they are the expressions of changes in the soul life of the earth. They have been described as "the earth's way of life" and this they are in a still further sense, for experience shows that the earth lives as a being of soul as truly as she exists as a body of rocks, stones, rivers and seas. Our human life of soul is by its inner nature related to the seasons because they originate in the soul of the earth. One has only to step out of the house and take a turn through the garden, to observe that the earth is not a thing but a creature with life. One has likewise, though this is not always realised, only to walk out on a day when spring is in the air, to perceive that the earth is a creature of soul as well as of life.

Men and women experience their personal life of soul in two alternating states, that of wakefulness and that of sleep. Awake, we are in ourselves, aware of thoughts and feelings, able to exercise our will to achieve our ends. Asleep, we are out of ourselves, the body lying quietly in bed, renewing its strength, the soul soaring away from the earth to journey through cosmic heights, gathering experience of which we are very little conscious. When we are asleep we neither think nor act; but out of the night's oblivion, wisdom is gathered that is discovered by the conscious mind on awakening. The earth likewise knows the alternating states of sleeping and waking but hers is a longer slower rhythm. In winter she concentrates her soul within herself as we do during the wakeful hours of daytime and in the summer months she breathes her soul out into the cosmos, as we do in sleep. She is wakeful in winter and dreamily sleeping in summer. When she breathes in, and her soul is within her body, her surface is bare and still, but below it she is very active. She is thinking deeply and her thoughts are sent down to her from the stars. When she breathes out, and her soul expands into the heights, her surface is covered with leaves, blossoms and a multitude of insects. She puts forth what she has thought in winter in the shape of growing, flowering things. In so doing, she passes into sleep and they become coloured, scented dreams. In spring she begins to breathe out her soul, and in autumn she begins to draw in her breath again. Waking and sleeping is a kind of breathing by which the soul is drawn in and breathed out again. As human beings we go through this process completely, from one existence to another, in twenty-four hours, but the earth takes twelve months and passes in this cycle through the four seasons, or, in other words, she wakes and sleeps, and so brings forth winter, spring, summer and autumn.

The states of sleeping and waking manifest the dual nature of the soul. It looks both ways, towards the world of earth and towards the world of the Heavens. It must pass to and fro between the two, or otherwise it would lose its existence either by being imprisoned in the sphere of matter or by being dissolved away in the heights of the spirit. The soul of man shares in the slow rhythm of the seasons as it does in the quicker alternations of day and night. In this way Mankind and the earth share their existence and follow in close relationship their way of life, in soul as much as in body. Both have the source of their existence in the Divine World in the heights. Both can fulfil their cosmic purpose only in separation from the Heavens, in withdrawal into the depths. So they lead a twofold existence, their strength being renewed in the heights, their wisdom evolved in the depths. They receive warmth and life from above, they find their own true purpose below. The seasons are their way of life which takes them both, Man and his Earth mother, from earth to Heaven and back again that the purpose of the world may come to fulfilment in the course of time.

THE FESTIVALS

The seasons manifest the changing course of the earth's life of soul. The Christian festivals, which are celebrated in conjunction with them, are the spiritual part of the year's round and are as necessary to it as they. Whereas, in living with the changes of the seasons, we human beings follow Nature, the celebration of the festivals depends on ourselves. The spiritual rhythm of the year is experienced and observed in sacred practices, which have their place in human life. In ancient times, before the beginning of Christianity, religious rites were performed in harmony with the changing relations of earth, sun and stars throughout the year. Since the Christian era began, the festivals honouring the coming of Christ, His death and His rising again, have likewise been held in accordance with the seasons. Out of a natural and right understanding, that has not failed until recent times, human beings have woven the web of their religious life on the loom of the year's rhythm of time.

In the sacred festivals of the religions older than Christianity outer and inner experiences were woven together. The practices of the Druids may serve as an illustration. Remains of their temples are still to be seen in places like Salisbury Plain, where Stonehenge stands, a circle made from enormous slabs of solid rock. Some of these stand upright, others are so arranged that two, side by side, are joined into a rough arch by another slab laid crosswise over the top. Together the stones form a circle set up in the centre of a wide stretch of plain. The sun's course through the sky would be visible at all times of the year and the shadows cast by the stones in its light would move with the seasons like the hands of a great clock laid on the ground. Temples of sun worship like these were places of communication between Heaven and earth. The priests were the interpreters of that which they read in the language of the moving constellations to the worshippers who gathered at the temple. In the coming chapters the theme of the stars and their significance for our human life will be taken up again. At this point one observation is relevant. In ancient religions, of which that of the Druids is but a single example, it was held that true wisdom was to be found by looking upwards to spheres of the Heavens, of which the outer indications are the stars. Religious practices were directed to asking for and receiving divine counsel, without which the people of those ages had no means of conducting their life on earth.

In their minds Heaven was not a vague term for a Paradise, to which good souls would go after death. It was a sphere of existence to which they looked up continually throughout their earthly lives, because they felt their daily dependence on its bounty. They knew as a matter of experience that they lived between two worlds. From birth to death they lived in the world of earth but they could still dimly recall the world of the Heavens, where their souls had dwelt before they were born. When they looked up to the sun and the stars, they felt that behind them lay the spheres, which they had once known. They were aware that a universe inhabited by beings, spiritual in their nature, divine in their qualities, had its existence invisible to earthly eyes in the Heavens. They worshipped when they beheld the stars the Divine World, from which they were separated on earth. They received from above gifts necessary to maintaining their life here below. The light and warmth of the sun, the life-giving virtue of the rain, the formative forces from the planets and stars they acknowledged as divine blessings. The impulses of thought, feeling and will within themselves they accepted as having flowed into them from the universe. When they sought wisdom and understanding, they turned to the Divine World, which they looked to find above and beyond their earthly dwelling. They did not expect to continue in existence without blessing and favour from above.

The Divine World, of which they were aware, is the reality, which in modern times is usually called God. A conception such as theirs is met with in the Gospels, though it is customary to pass this over. In the sayings of Jesus Christ, God is often spoken of as "the Kingdom of Heaven". In earlier times, it was as natural to people to think of living worlds, as today it is for us to speak in terms of persons. A decisive change has come about since then. In the times before Christianity outer and inner experience was much the same. The world around was accepted as the work of divine powers. They were apprehended behind the outer appearance which surrounded them like garments. People looked up to the sun in the sky and beheld the shining form of the god who lived there in company with the lesser beings, who did him service. Today we look into the world around and above us and regard only its appearance. When we seek the Divine Spirit we look, not outside, but within. We worship the reality of God, apart from His creation where we see His handiwork but not His presence.

The turning point of our history was the coming of Christ. Through Him the new direction was initiated. We feel this when we stand in an ancient holy place like Stonehenge and consider how different was the religious experience of those who worshipped there from our own. We find it described in the Bible, when we compare the Old Testament with the New, when we listen inwardly to Jehovah speaking to His people and Christ talking to His followers. In the coming chapters a further description will be given of how the chosen Hebrew people prepared for the coming of the Messiah. The heathen religions of those times likewise made ready for His advent, each after their own fashion and their part will be included. When He appeared for whom all nations and races had so long waited with hope, He came to make all things new. He did not restore that which had gone before and was ready to die. He brought the source of new spiritual life and power, choosing for its shrine the inner place within the souls of men. More on this theme will be said in later pages. Here the bare fact is sufficient that the whole nature of human spiritual life was changed. Whereas earlier human beings had found the divine presence outside themselves, shining down to them from the Heavens above and reflected back to them from the surrounding world of Nature, from henceforth they were to hear the still small voice speak from within. Christ brought the indwelling Spirit to human souls on earth and in so doing changed the state of their whole existence. It has been often said of Him that He founded a new religion. He did much more. He initiated the greatest change in evolution since the world began. He commenced the process, which is still unfinished today, of making anew the nature of Man and the being of the earth. His coming is a fact written deep into the history of the world.

Since Christianity began, those who have followed it have learnt to turn their attention to the Spirit dwelling within the soul. In concentrating upon this sphere of experience they have lost the memory of the ancient wisdom, which those people found in earlier ages who looked above and around them to seek the presence of God. It is true that today the divine voice speaks within. But it is still a reality that the realm of Nature, which we inhabit, reflects the divine wisdom that has reigned since the creation of the world. It is likewise a lasting truth that the star-filled universe above is the veil behind which is hidden the Divine World by whose blessing we live and have our being as in ancient times. In the present age Christianity should attain a further development. In past centuries it was necessary for Christian souls to learn slowly to follow the new direction of spiritual life and to turn inwards in search of the Spirit. Now they should have grown spiritually mature enough to reach out from within to the Spirit of God that works in the realms of the Heavens and has left His image in the world around. Christianity has become a personal faith and should now develop further into a cosmic religion. Those who have found the light of Christ within should seek His light also in the world without.

Christianity becomes cosmic in character when the festivals of the Christian year are celebrated in true harmony with the intercourse between earth and Heaven which is expressed in the changing seasons. An old tradition has caused certain customs to be preserved in the Churches to this effect, although such usages are not comprehensible to many people nowadays. But the Christian religion will not enter upon a new stage of development through the observance of old customs. A new understanding is needed for the meaning of these festivals and a new appreciation for the spiritual rhythms in the earth's life. Then we shall discover for ourselves in our inner life that the way through the round of seasons and festivals is a path of Christian experience for the soul. The coming chapters of this book will follow the course of this path.

The cycle of festivals begins at Advent and passes, in the winter half of the year, through Christmas, Epiphany, Lent, Easter and Ascension. At Whitsuntide, as the first half is completed, the second begins, and the summer festivals of St John's tide and Michaelmas follow. Studies on each of these festivals will be found later in the book, in which the attempt is made to describe side by side the mood in Nature and the character of the Christian experience belonging particularly to this time. Interspersed between these studies, chapters will be found on subjects from the Gospels on which our minds can fittingly dwell at each of the festival seasons. Each one will find his own way along the path of experience leading through the Christian year. Those who make a practice for a long while of following in their inner life the course of the festivals will find that Christianity becomes an evermore living and growing reality within them. We cannot say in truth that we are already Christians. We can resolve to continue year by year growing in grace to become Christians. In the changing rhythms of the festivals we find the opportunity for growth and becoming.

What is said in this book originates from the discoveries made about Christianity by Rudolf Steiner. We live today in an age of discoveries but many of those which are best known are scientific and mechanical. Religion is a field in which we do not easily expect them but they are there. Christianity is not a finished product of the past to be accepted by tradition. It is a living growing faith with a long future before it, which is due for an important phase of development in the present. Rudolf Steiner discovered in the early part of this century much that is necessary for the new understanding and practice of Christianity. Part of what he found had been known in earlier times and forgotten. Part is new discovery belonging to the present age. All the wisdom he gave was expressed through the consciousness of a modern scientific mind. His way of thinking about Christianity is in itself a discovery, through which many a person of today can find comprehension and faith. He was the pioneer in the modern age of spiritual discovery.

From Rudolf Steiner's conception of Christianity appears the idea that is the guiding thought of the studies to follow. Before He descended to earth, Christ dwelt in the spiritual realm of the sun. He was the inspiring genius of the planet, who is king among the others, whose outer face shines with light and warmth upon the earth. The ancient people who worshipped the sun, knew this and were addressing in their prayers the being of Christ in the existence He had in Heaven before He reached the earthly world. When He became man, He left His heavenly dwelling and since that time the divine Spirit of the sun has united Himself with the life of the earth. When the sun looks down from the sky, he is seeking the most precious part of his being here below. The earth holds a treasure of light within her through which she will in times to come shine like a spiritual sun. This theme will be taken up again and again as in the round of festivals the being of Christ is seen from different sides.

This idea shows us the inner reason why the Christian festivals should be celebrated in harmony with the seasons. Christ is spiritually related to the living being of both the sun and the earth. Their communion with each other in the course of the year takes place in a sphere where He can be present. Christmas could not be rightly celebrated at any season but midwinter, nor St John's tide at any but midsummer. Easter has its proper place in the spring, Michaelmas in the autumn. Through the cycle of the festivals, as they follow one after the other, the picture of Christ is revealed to the eyes of our souls. We should not be able to comprehend it, if we should behold the whole in one moment. When the vision is spread out over the festivals of the year, we see Him first from one side, then another. What we can see and comprehend at Christmas is not the same as at Easter. What we perceive at St John's tide is carried further and fulfilled at Michaelmas. If one would ask oneself, how can I best find Him? one could answer: I shall find him where He is revealed to me in the changing course of the seasons, through them I shall comprehend how His working is unfolded. The earth has received Him into the changing life of her seasons and shows Him to human souls. The Light of the World is not far off in the Heavens. He is here in our midst on earth.

ADVENT

ADVENT

Advent is the time of looking forward and waiting. One cycle of the Christian year has just come to an end. On the first Sunday in Advent the new round of the festivals begins once more. This is not the beginning of the year according to the calendar or the reckoning of dates for ordinary life. The Christian year and the calendar start from different points, though both cover the cycle of twelve months. They measure time in a different manner. In the calendar all the days have equal length, and, though some may be marked in red because they are public holidays, they will have the same number of hours and minutes. Yet everyone of us who looks into a new, empty diary knows that the days will not be all equal. There will be some very eventful ones, others quiet or dull, some full of great decisions or experiences, others occupied only with daily duties. We know that we will find as the days go by our own especial year of experience unrolling. In the Christian year the passing of time is also not always the same. But its rhythm is not, like the individual year of experience, different for each person, it is the same for everyone. It moves between high points of festival and periods leading up to or away from them. Its time is reckoned by quality, whereas that of the calendar is counted in terms of quantity.

The movements of the sun and the stars in relation to the earth determine the course of the Christian year, but each of its festivals reveals part of the content of Christianity. The year begins just before the natural turning point of midwinter. It starts quietly with a season of preparation, of waiting, of listening for what is to come. It begins, like the day, with a quiet period of twilight in which the sky grows brighter and the early light gradually seeps through the grey of night, until the dusk is at last filled with the mighty glow of the sun's rising. Advent is the twilight which comes before the sunrise of Christmas. The mood of this time is quiet contemplation. The great truth of Christ's coming will be the theme of Christmas. It can be taken up in thought and pondered in the heart during the four weeks of preparation. The sense of expectancy increases as the thoughts deepen. The mood of anticipation gives the season its special character.

Is anticipation the sweetest part of any experience? There are moments when one may be tempted to think so, for anticipation makes one somewhat of a visionary. In looking forward to something that has not yet happened, one sees the ideal picture of what is to come. One reads prophetically in the Spirit what is about to come down to earth. When it arrives some of the glow of the ideal has been lost, the earthly conditions have made their mark too strongly. Nevertheless, when one comes later into the mood of anticipation again, the aroma is as delicately sweet as ever. There is no deception in this sweetness, for the ideal pictures are true in the worlds of Spirit, though their earthly reflection may be blurred. Therein lies the source of true hope, the feeling that grows out of anticipation in Advent. Hope, though it may be fulfilled only in part, or not at all, is kindled by true realities of the Spirit. Their existence is lasting and they give continual promise of good influences sent down to the world of Earth. To deny hope is to deny the power of the Spirit itself. The Christian year begins with a season of quietude, when the soul lifts up its thoughts to contemplate the Heavens and to be filled with hope in the everlasting might and goodness of God.

Contemplation, expectancy, hope, all weave the mood of Advent in the soul. There is quiet also outside in the realm of

Nature. The leaves have fallen, the land lies bare to the sky. The seeds are underground and Nature's activity is concentrated under the surface of the soil. When no winter storms are actually in process, the air becomes very still and the sky looks down calmly. The sky was more vivid in the summer, but at the beginning of winter it is often filled with many colours, gentle in hue and spread out softly through its wide expanse. It looks as if a rainbow had been melted and had flowed out to fill the dome of the Heavens. Sometimes, when sun and rain meet in the right manner, a winter rainbow actually appears in strong colours. Then the inner mood of the season and the outer event are at one. The rainbow is the token of Advent. The seven colours that shine there, clearly distinguished from one another, are a reflection of the sun's beams in which all the colours are melted into one blaze of light. The rainbow is the offspring of the sun and its herald. Furthermore, it is also the interpreter of the sun's light, revealing the pure nature of the colours, which are born out of the shining of the light into the darkness. The secrets of creation have their sign in the rainbow. It is a true token of hope and promise. As such it appeared, for the first time, to Noah, after the ending of the great flood. Since then human eyes behold in its radiance the sign of the creating power of God. Towards that of which it speaks our thoughts are turned in the quiet days of Advent.

The true spiritual mood of this season, which has just been described, does not come about quite without human effort. There is much in the world that will help the heart to feel it, but there is also much to hinder. Just as winter storms often obscure the calm sky at this time, so those who try to foster this mood in themselves will often meet storms from outside to shake their inner quiet. This season is one of struggle and its tranquillity will often have to be won in face of disturbance. All the hindrances arise that could make hard and difficult the coming of Christmas as a spiritual event. Foremost among them is the commercial Christmas of the present day, drawing the interest of people to outer things, filling the quiet with material distractions. The old customs which are exploited in business at this season had originally a spiritual meaning, but their sense is nowadays made quite external. This is not, however, the only kind of hindrance. Struggles between people, disturbances in destiny, often occur just in these weeks, which are rarely uneventful in ordinary life. The forces against quiet and peace of mind are out to shatter the true mood of Advent. Strength of will is needed to renew tranquillity again and again, from within, against discouragement. Advent is not to be experienced without effort.

The content of Advent as a Christian festival is twofold. Our thoughts go back to the ages of time before the coming of Christ to earth, when this event was prepared. The mystery of the world's creation is the first theme that belongs naturally to this season. The inner eye of the mind looks back in contemplation to the beginning. The vision unfolds of the Godhead concentrated inwards, meditating, brooding over the things to come. When the divine pondering reached a certain intensity, it began to flow over into the activity of creation. So long as the meditative silence of God reigned, the Godhead was one and individual. When the flow of time began to move and the divine silence changed into the outpouring of creative power, a distinction appeared within the Being of God. The pondering silence, in which all creation was gathered together and prepared, revealed the Being of the Father-god. The creative energy streaming out to form, shape, ensoul and bring to birth the created world, revealed the Being of the Son-god. The world-silence is the realm of the Father, the world-speaking is the presence of the Son, who is the Word of God. In the stream of creation all beings and created things came forth from God and received life. Man was born with the created world and in the first stage of his existence he was sheltered within the divine Being. In the radiant working of the universe Man began to live his own human life as the youngest creature brought forth from the World of God.

A shadow crossed the glory of this dawn. There were already present in the universe beings who had rebelled against the divine order, whose will had become evil. They sought entry into this newly created world and it was allowed to them. The devil came in and brought temptation to Man, who was too young and incomplete in his nature to resist. It came about in consequence that the world of God and the world in which Man henceforth had to live out his existence on earth broke asunder. The created world fell away from the Heavens and became a place where the powers of evil could work. The being of Man was changed by their influence, losing more and more of the divine image, being increasingly infected with the curse of death. The creation of the world and the fall into evil are the powerful facts of world history that naturally belong to our contemplation in Advent. To enter deeply into what happens at Christmas, it is essential to have first filled the heart and mind with the thoughts of what preceded the coming of Christ. During Advent we contemplate the way in which the Divine World has guided the history of Mankind. We look back in order to read the mind of God reflected in the events on earth.

The content of Advent is not all to be found in looking back. No Christian festival is only filled with the remembrance of what one has been. It contains a living, present content of quite as much significance. Christ has worked in the past. He lives and works as really and as potently in the present and will do so in all times to come. How does His presence now appear before our inner eyes in Advent? Once in the past Christ came from the Heavens down to the earth. Now in the present century He comes again. But there is an essential difference in His coming. He has in fact, since the deed He wrought on Golgotha through crucifixion and resurrection, never left the earth. His Spirit is continuously present in this world, inspiring and guiding the history of Mankind.

How then can He come again? Though present, He is not always manifest to the souls of men and women with the same clarity. The stars in the sky are a likeness for this. They are always there, night and day, yet we speak of them as "coming out" in the dusk. They are not visible, though present, by day, but they become visible as darkness falls. When the presence of Christ, which is constantly with us, becomes visible, it may be said that He comes again. In no sense does it mean that He takes on today an existence in the body, as He did in Palestine when He became man in Jesus. That has happened once and there is no need for it to be repeated, since that which was to be achieved through this event was fulfilled. The new coming is a revelation of His Being to the eyes and the minds of men and women. To some He manifests Himself as cosmic Life sounding as the music of the spheres. Many may feel His inner presence in their own hearts. Some in the present and many in the future will see Him coming to meet them from outside. In such moments the eyes of those who see behold a human figure, but their hearts perceive that more than another person stands before them. He appears as a spiritual Being clad in the likeness of a human being. They see Him with earthly eyes and yet at that moment their eyes are opened by a more than common spiritual insight. The meeting with the visible presence of Christ is the sign for a great expansion of His working and influence on our world today. The upheavals that daily beset us all the world over are the disturbance caused by this event. As at His first coming the devils were the first to recognise Him, so it is again now.

CREATION AND FALL

In the time of Advent the world becomes still and hushed. Outwardly the bustle may be greater than ever, for the Christmas holiday demands preparation, but the true inner need of the season is quiet and tranquil. Our thoughts turn to the deepest facts of existence and we cease for a moment to take for granted the world around, in which we live and move. We look into the depths of being, to all that which upholds what we are, which gives substantial basis to our thinking and doing. We apprehend the ground of all existence and recognise the divine forces present in all that maintains and preserves us. Our life is founded in the being of God and preserved by the bounty continually flowing to us from His hands.

The world around is the mirror wherein we see Him reflected. The ground underfoot is firm, the hills preserve their mass and contour so long that they outlast the memory of generations. All things that have shape but are without life are the enduring foundation of our changing existence. They firmly resist our touch: they keep the forms in which they are fixed. Their will has become lasting endurance, giving to our activity the fixed background without which we could do nothing. In this experience we perceive God as the ground of all existence, on whom we rest, whose unchanging will is the foundation of all our being.

Living things take root in the soil. Securely anchored in the ground, they send up their shoots and spread their branches. They have their being in continual change, never the same today as yesterday, and tomorrow becoming different again. Ceaselessly they move through the cycle of growth and decay to new life. They thrive on the forces from above, the falling rain, the shining light, the ripening warmth. The coming and going between the heights and the depths is maintained by the divine power of the universe. The process by which Spirit becomes visible matter and then returns again whence it came, continues to renew the earth's existence.

The breathing, moving creatures go to and fro upon the ground. They have an inner life of feeling to which the plants do not attain. In them the world becomes experience, intensely felt, strongly moved between the opposites of joy and grief, pleasure and pain, boldness and fear. Their energy carries them over the earth's wide spaces in the joy of continual activity and abounding life. The divine powers of soul in the universe breathe through the existence of the moving creatures on the earth. Their life is likewise of God.

In stone, plant and beast we see His reflection. Within ourselves also we see and know it. We have a mineral, vegetable and animal portion in our nature, which surrounds and enfolds the truly human part as the husk holds the kernel of the nut. Within and around us we perceive the working of God and see His image. Once, at the beginning of time, when the world was created, it was within and one with God. In the silence of the All, the divine Word came forth and began to speak. The Son, in whom the creative power of the Divine World had concentrated and ripened, proceeded from the Father, after the manner in which the word is brought forth from the heart and the lips of him who speaks. The universal substance of God was revealed in creation through the activity of the Son, who in due time became Christ. When the act of creating was performed at the beginning, the Divine Being, who was revealed, was at one with the revelation of Himself. As the open face of a person expresses the living soul behind it, so the created universe showed forth the glory of the Creator. Creation was spoken forth from the mind of God, but not made independent and separate in the speaking. By comparison, it might be said that, if a speaker would speak and remain one with what is spoken, giving life and reality to the words, so it was at the beginning of the universe. The Word of God spoke and was Himself that which was spoken. God experienced His own being, manifesting it in revelation of Himself.

Since then the created world has become His image. The Divine Word has become a memory, which we see around us in the ground beneath, the starry sky above, in the lifeless stones, the living plants and the creatures who breathe and are ensouled. The ordered, beautiful and, in a sense, still world, where we dwell, is the work of God and manifests His being, but does so like a memorial, like something from the past that is finished and done. What has made the glorious creation of the beginning into a remembered image?

God made the world and saw that it was good. Last among the creatures He made was the one in whom the whole divine image was concentrated and reflected, Man. Many divine beings are members of the one being of God, in whom the universe exists and rests. They in community brought forth the idea of Man, bestowing upon him the manifold qualities and virtues from their own diverse natures. All should be expressed in one creature, who should be as manifold as they, and yet a unity, as the ultimate Godhead Himself is the united Whole. Though the last to take on separate form, Man is in origin the firstborn of creation, since in him is comprehended all that is divinely manifested in the other creatures. The pattern of his being is the divine universe itself. In him is the small world, reflecting the great, from which he was brought forth at the beginning, when Man was made in the image of God. As the human soul turns in thought to the origin of human existence, reverence wells up for the idea of Man formed in the mind of God. Man is the offspring of the heavenly hosts, who fashioned him in the divine likeness, that he might reveal in himself the one almighty God, in whom they live, move and have their being.

Before the divine pattern had been fulfilled in the first human souls, while they were unfinished and without the inner strength of selfhood, they were attacked by the beings of evil. They, in contrast to the other sons of God, had powers of willing divided from the Divine Will. In the process of Man's creation they were able to act separately from the community of their fellows, who were enclosed within the universal Will. They interfered in human existence and changed Man's nature. From two directions the beings came who entangled human souls with evil. He first came whose ancient name is Lucifer and offered the apple from the forbidden tree, which gave knowledge of good and evil. The senses awoke in the newborn souls, but their gaze was turned towards the world outside. Before this happened, hearing, seeing, touching and all the other organs of sense were open to perceive directly the living, weaving energies of the divine beings labouring at the task of creation. Afterwards, the eyes, ears, and hands of humans lost the gift of spiritual perception and could only experience the world of created things, in which the hardening process of death had begun to work.

In the beginning the human souls had been united with the universe in which they had been enfolded. After they had become part of the fallen world they began to become aware of themselves as separate beings. They felt the first impulses of longing and fear. They realised dimly, and then more clearly, their own independent will. Once the will of the Creator had penetrated their every part, then they began to feel the pulsing of will-force, separate, individual and estranged from the ordering of God.

From the opposite direction came the other great prince of evil, called by the old name of Ahriman. He condensed Man's being and that of the world into the state of matter, to which he gave the force of reality. The first creation was not material and was without death. The later, fallen condition of all created things was infected with the sting of death. Whereas before, they had been made of the substance of life and immortal, they became material and subject to decay. The hardened state of reality that is natural today began then to exist, produced by the fall into sin. This second power of evil laid hold on Man's nature and caused it to shrink and shrivel. Man, created offspring of the universe, to reflect its image in himself, became through Ahriman's influence able only to express his own small being. He began to speak, not the words of God, but the language of himself and his limited existence.

When Man fell into separation from the Divine World, the realm of earth fell with him. The creating God ceased to be one with creation and withdrew His immediate presence to the Heavens. The earthly world became separated from the divine realms, and the dividing wall between them became denser and harder to surmount through the course of ages. Such a state of things did not come about in a moment of time. A trend of evolution, a tendency to separation into two worlds of existence, was started with the first act of interference by the beings of evil. In consequence, the living together as one of Creator and creature, of God, Man and the world, of the divine spheres of the Spirit with the realm they had brought forth, began to disappear. The universe divided, and Man came into a state of division within himself, split into a twofold nature, heavenly and earthly, alternating between two kinds of existence, that within the body and that without the body.

The world around us has grown firm and still as the trend of evolution progressed which began with the Fall. Gradually through the ages it has become the memorial of God, the Creator of all things. It is still fed continuously from above with the forces of life, without which it would become a corpse. Nevertheless, the Divine Presence has long ago withdrawn, leaving an image behind which still reflects the being of God as a memory from the beginning. Such an interference with His creation must have been willingly endured by God Himself. Anything other were unthinkable, when one contemplates the nature of the highest Godhead. Within the Divine World, beings were allowed to emerge, gifted with forces of willing separated from the order of heavenly existence. They were not prevented from exercising their independent will in the unfinished being of Man. They were not hindered from making the earthly world into a place where they could become active outside the harmonious order of the Heavens. They could make themselves princes of this fallen world and constant tempters of human souls while they are its inhabitants.

God suffers the power of evil to exert the force of will contrary to His and to establish the reality of death in the universe. Difficult as it is for human thought to conceive of this, nevertheless evil is a fact of world-existence that has come into being and been granted a sphere in which to unfold its mysterious activity. Among the mysteries of the universe, that of evil is one of the most difficult to comprehend. Where is the answer to this riddle? Is it not found in that aspect of the divine nature, in order to contemplate which we have to enlarge our imagination? The source of creation is with God and has been from the beginning before evil yet was. Even the activity of beings who are turned against the divine order is absorbed into the boundless creative Will of the Kingdom of Heaven. If evil were abolished by God, nothing but its destruction would result. When it is absorbed into evolution, the Power that created the world will in time transform what is dark, what is lost, what works against the divine purposes of the present, into fruits that will be able to ripen in eternity.

When the influences of the princes of evil began to interfere in the existence of human souls, Man's nature began to change. The image of God in him was gradually obscured and distorted. The innocent soul that had at first been his became infected with the sickness of sin. He became capable of exerting the independent will that had been given to him out of due time, before he could use it rightly, to harm and to destroy. He began to treat as the only true reality the realm of matter which his shrunken organs of sense showed him. Slowly but surely he became blind of heart and limited of mind. He fell ever further into the danger of being disintegrated in his whole nature and failing his true destiny.

Although the divine idea of Man became ever more and more distorted in men and women as the ages of history progressed, one capacity developed within them as a result of their loneliness from God, the sense of being a self, individual and distinct, with their own power of willing, gradually emerged in human souls. The condition in which freedom could be evolved developed from the isolation of Mankind. But freedom was not yet recognised as a human ideal. The sense of self had the effect of throwing the soul into the deepest darkness, cutting it off from God and from other human beings. Happiness and strength were drawn from being merged without distinction into the community of the tribe and family. The quality of being a self was held to be derived from sin, self-will and rebellion against the Divine Will. Those who attained it were threatened with death and final rejection by the Heavens.

Nevertheless, freedom was already an idea in the mind of God. That which most divided human souls from the divine presence would become the seed of a quality not yet born in any of God's creatures. Man, through his separation, might become the firstborn of a new creation. This could never come about unaided. Left to the impetus of evolution since the Fall, Man could only descend further towards death and be lost to the universe. The mood in the souls of men and women in the time before the coming of Christ became more tragic from age to age. On earth no help was to be found as the power of the old religions grew increasingly weaker. Help could come only from the Heavens. Would the creating power of God be wielded again to rescue His creatures?

INCARNATION AND
SECOND COMING

Among the Sons of God in the heights of the Heavens there was concern and sorrow over the plight of Man in the darkened, fallen realm of Earth. The youngest child of their creation, into whose nature the forces of worlds had been poured, no longer reflected the divine image clearly. Man had become the lost son of the Father in the Heavens. The earth was falling into the cold grip of death and the ceaseless conflict of the opposing powers of evil was consuming human existence. The Sons of God turned their gaze upon the dark place in the universe, which had fallen away from their dominion, and they were filled with compassion. They were moved by the will to bring healing to the lost children of men, to send life where death reigned and light where darkness prevailed. Among the divine community a world-decision was formed and matured. It was resolved to send means of salvation to mankind on earth, to give One from the highest Godhead to descend as healer into the god-forsaken realm. He through whom the creating Word of God had poured forth creation at the beginning took upon Himself the task of salvation.

He was not impelled to this resolve by any necessity from within His own nature. Human souls descend at birth into existence in this world because their destiny can only be fulfilled here. They belong by their very nature to the life of the earth. Their way of evolution can only be continued in the conditions prevailing in this sphere. The force of necessity impels their eternal souls past the gate of birth down into incarnation, right into the midst of the experiences and dangers of this world. The descent of Christ came about in quite another manner. It was resolved in freedom and done as an act of grace in response to the desperate need of Mankind. God Himself sent His Son to seek the lost child of the Heavens in the far country where he was threatened with disintegration and death. The Son came in the strength of free will, out of compassion for the helpless children of men, to perform for them the deed of saving grace.

He descended into a human body to live for a short time the life of a man on earth. The Son of God did not come in divine majesty, with the powers of the universe at His command. He accepted human existence, limiting Himself to the narrow bounds of a human soul and body. Although, when He came, there was great expectation among people of the long foretold coming of a god to bring the solution to the tragic dilemma of Mankind, very few recognised Him as the One in whom the prophecies were fulfilled. The greater number were looking for a god who would show himself to them in the exercise of might and magnificence. What they who walked with Him on earth actually beheld was a Being whose divine qualities were manifested in restraint, in the resignation of His powers. They found it very difficult to understand how He who had come to save them could achieve His purpose in this manner. His aim was beyond their grasp. He had come to help Mankind find the rightful path of destiny, to save human souls from wandering astray, from falling by the roadside before the destination could be reached. He had not come to spare people the need for further evolution, to rescue them from the temptations and struggles of earthly life. Salvation was not sent ready-made from the Heavens to end all tribulation. Christ came to bring new meaning to human life, to give a new impulse to the evolving destiny of

Mankind. He turned the tragedy of Man's existence, beset by beings who work evil and menaced by the power of death, into the opportunity to achieve salvation in the long struggle that will only be finished at the end of history.

No human soul understands without great inner effort the purpose with which the Son of God descended from the Heavens into the existence of Man on earth. Human thinking has to raise itself to the thinking of God, the heart has to be lifted up to listen to the heart of God, before the soul can comprehend intentions brought down from the mind of the Divine Father. The herald of Christ, John the Baptist, cried continually to his hearers: "Change your hearts and minds". If his hearers were to recognise and understand Him who was to come, they must have changed their minds and cleared their hearts of wishes and assumptions. How could they otherwise perceive the purpose of One who was to behave and act out of the mind of God, who came not to answer the expectations of the people, but to do the will of God?

This has been at all times since the necessary preparation for understanding the work of Christ. He is not to be understood by those who approach Him with heart and mind unchanged, with eyes confused by earthly considerations. His purpose is as little to be comprehended now as it was then, without this change. The heart has to be prepared to ask: what aim and intention has the Son of God brought with Him from the heights of Heaven to the realm of earth? What has changed in the purpose of Man's destiny because He has entered human life and Himself become man?

Before His coming, human beings felt in the depths of their being a conviction that they had fallen from that which they should have become, that they were untrue to the pattern of their humanity. When they sought what they remembered but felt they had lost, they looked back down the generations of their ancestors, through the past courses of time, to the beginning of Mankind's existence. There, at the creation, they found the divine image of Man, brought forth in its original purity from the being of the Godhead. They knew in the depths of their heart that Man is in truth that which he was created at the beginning, but his divine image has become only a memory. Once human beings lived near to God, and their lives were overshadowed by His presence. Since then they have been separated from Him, and the remembrance of the divine image has faded in the course of time.

Such was the experience of those who lived before the coming of the Messiah. An example of how they endeavoured to find what was lost is to be found in the early part of St Luke's Gospel, in the third chapter, where the family tree of Jesus of Nazareth is described. A list of names is given, beginning with Joseph and going backwards through all the preceding generations until it ends with Adam "who was the son of God". These names, which mean little today, signified then the great men of the past, who represented the succeeding ages of history. They called up a series of pictures for contemplation, which led the mind back along the tragic path of human destiny to the light at the beginning, when the first man was the Son of God.

In the ages before the coming of Christ piety meant preserving in one's inner and outer life, with all one's might, the original image of Man. Every thought, word and deed unworthy of it was sinful and impious. As the effects of Man's original fall into separation from the Divine World increased, piety weakened and faded in the sin-sickened souls of men. When Christ came, He did not condemn and destroy all that had become unworthy in Man's nature. Had He done so, little would have been left. Nor did He change Man by the magic of His divine, cosmic powers. Had He done so, the human being would have become an empty puppet moved on strings pulled by the will of God. No divine force would have dwelt within his soul. Christ accepted Man's fallen nature and opened up before human understanding the prospect of change from within, of salvation to be attained by long effort through future ages of evolution. He called upon men and women to open wide the eyes of their souls to see ahead the ideal of what they should become. Earlier, they had looked back in tragic regret for the divine image created at the beginning. Now they were to change the direction of their gaze and look on to the future. They were to behold the true pattern of Humanity shining in the distance of times to come, an aim to be reached, a purpose to be fulfilled.

Once already the ideal of Man has been made real and actual. It happened when Jesus Christ walked on earth and revealed in Himself, through word and deed, the divine image in human form. He became that which those who follow Him will become when the work of transforming their being in every part is accomplished and they are made Christ-like. When today we read the Gospels, we are not only reading the history of something that once took place. We are in fact looking into the future, finding, in the mirror of His life, the ideal, which every human soul may behold and take for his own.

Christ came to show to men and women the way of salvation that leads through coming ages of evolution. But human souls were weak and disintegrated: how could they hope to tread such a way in the midst of so many temptations? The beings of God in the heights of Heaven had seen into what depths of misery and sin Mankind had fallen. Their Messenger did not come to teach impossible aims. He came to make the spiritual ideal of Man into the inspiring reality in the lives of men and women on earth. He did this by sacrificing Himself into the earthly destiny of Mankind. He performed in this world the deed which changed the course of history, which made the new way of evolution into a living fact. The divine, cosmic powers, which He restrained while He lived as Jesus in the body and soul of a man, were poured out in the deed of the cross, when He entered into death and rose again to life.

Fresh forces to quicken her existence flowed into the living being of the earth, which had been threatened with decay and dissolution. Spiritual power entered the being of Mankind, giving to human souls the energy and strength to enter upon the new age of evolution. Christ rose again from death on earth and is present in spirit since that time with human souls in the struggle of existence. He is Himself the way of salvation. He treads it with us, He points to the aim and end, He awakens the ideal in our hearts. The life of this world is in His care, for He has taken it upon Himself. He has not appeared once for a short time on earth and left Mankind to struggle on alone. He has made His own existence into the living way of salvation, taking the tribulation of the world for His lot, giving from the wellspring of His Spirit new life to the souls of men.

When we look in the present time into the state of the world in which we dwell, we may well say: is Christ really present? How can such things be? He did not come at His incarnation to change the world by magic, nor does He do today what He would not do then. His presence can be glimpsed in the returning life that quickens at midwinter in the earth and will bring forth the new season of spring. The earth would long ago have died, man would long ago have destroyed or would destroy her now, but for His care.

His presence can be found too in the human heart. Human nature has not become wholly good nor free from temptation. Nevertheless, in such unworthy dwellings as our weak and sickened souls, this Spirit has chosen to live. Looking within, we find not one self, but two. The one is our ordinary personality, in which we cannot avoid recognising much egotism and self-seeking. We feel the longing to overcome this part of ourselves and to transform it into something more worthy. The higher self, which is discovered when we seek deeper into our being, is that through which we are able from time to time to overcome the other and to transform our inner nature. It is the Spirit that creates from within, whose mysterious power is still only known to us in part. In every impulse of selflessness, in each effort to become self-responsible, in all our acts of self-control, we are aware that a divine being has found a place within the human soul.

The work of the indwelling Spirit is that which should create us again in the future image of Man and should change the world by the effort of evolution into the kingdom of Christ. Once human beings looked up to the Spirit of God beyond and outside them. Moses received the Law written by the divine finger on tablets of stone for the guidance and education of his people. Elijah listened in the storm, the earthquake and the fire for the Lord's voice. He expected to find His presence outside in the mighty forces of nature, where from the beginning He had appeared. A new experience came to him, a little prophecy of the quiet world revolution which would come with the Messiah, and he found the Lord speaking with a still, small voice within his heart. Christ's coming is a fact inscribed in human nature for all to read who will understand.

The chaos we see around us is produced by a vast process of decline in the world. The time has come when much that was brought forth in the past can no longer continue. Dark clouds of destruction roll over the scene of history and human beings are often swept into the process, increasing its force. Against this dark background the bright light of Christ's presence shines out into the world of men. Those who wish to work for the creation of what should come, to foster the new life that should grow up from the ashes of what is gone, find in Him the source of creating power. It is easy to see with our ordinary eyes the destruction around us. It is hard to see the seed of new life quickening in its midst. Only when the eye of the soul is opened in faith can our minds begin to see visions of that which the Spirit of Christ performs here and now in our presence. The light that shines in the darkness is revealed again in a new dawn.

CHRISTMAS

CHRISTMAS

How long does Christmas last? When Boxing Day is over people can be heard asking each other: have you had a good Christmas? The custom has arisen of treating the 24th, 25th and 26th of December as if they were the whole festival. Certainly two of these days are usually public holidays, at least in England. Nevertheless, Christmas is in reality a fact of the cosmos, of the life of the earth and the stars. There are therefore twelve days and thirteen nights of this holy season, which begins in the night of Christmas Eve and lasts until the festival of the Three Kings on January 6th. Many old carols mention the tradition of these days and nights, which gradually was forgotten after the Reformation.

Though forgotten, it is still a reality. We can discover this for ourselves, if we observe the character of these days. After the 6th of January we will find a change in what we can feel and observe. In the days before, we will be able to experience a particular quiet over the earth. This is not the quiet of anticipation, as in Advent, but the stillness in which a great cosmic happening takes place, which must not be disturbed. The Heavens are nearest to the earth, nearer than at any other season, so close that they bend down over the still, dark land. The sky in these days, delicate in colour, glows with a clear light of blessing. It is not difficult to apprehend this, if one accepts any chance of turning aside from the world's bustle and noise to watch and listen. At night the nearness of the Heavens can be felt even more clearly through the soft darkness or in the shining of the stars, when they are to be seen. Underneath all changes of weather the tone of the holy time can be felt steadily continuing. The heart can feel: Christmas is happening in very truth.

The turning earthward of the sun is the great event in the sky. Ever since midsummer, the sun has been withdrawing from the earth, the days have shortened. The world has grown colder and darker. It is the midnight of the year. Then comes the turning point. The shortest day is past and the sun begins to turn earthward again, with the promise of light, warmth and life renewed. The new birth of the sun has come, and its light fills human hearts. The mood of joy and goodwill, which people feel should be especially abroad at this season, could be described as the state in which each heart shines with sunlight. Just at the time of year when outwardly the world is coldest and darkest, the sun comes into our feeling. In ancient times, there was a spiritual experience, to which some of the great human souls attained. It was said of them that they saw the sun at midnight. In the outer darkness of the night, they could follow in visions the course of the sun's journey, but as they looked they were aware of his spiritual being in a way they could never achieve by observing his outer appearance in the sky by day. In another sense, nowadays, we see the sun at midnight in Christmas time. The spiritual being of the sun becomes clearer to our hearts, when our eyes see little of his beams outside.

One of the thoughts which belong to the contemplations of this season is that of the light. The human heart has a great longing for light, both from without and from within. All our awareness of what is around, of ourselves, all our understanding comes from light. It shows us the wonder and beauty of the universe. The created world around is the product of its working in the darkness. Light and darkness together weave the tapestry of that which our eyes see. Our longing for light is mingled with the desire for warmth and for life. We expect these gifts from the sun, which gives to all alike, good, bad and indifferent, the wealth of its gifts.

What is the spiritual wealth of the sun? It is love. In the tireless giving we feel the spirit of love shining forth in light, warmth and life. When thought penetrates at last to the spirit of the sun, there is found the revelation of Christ. He it is in whom the sun's essence lives. He it is whose descent into the darkness of earth is celebrated at Christmas. He is the bringer of light that is love.

On Christmas night the experience comes again into our hearts of the spirit-sun born into the darkness of earth at the midnight hour of the world. Christ left His heavenly dwelling in the sun to come into the earth, that the souls of human beings might not be lost altogether in the darkness and the struggle with evil. The sun continues to shine in the sky and to be the source of life for the earth. Yet when the planet above us seeks its own spirit, the true source of his being, he no longer finds it within himself but outside, beyond, far away on the earth. Christ carried the sun's spirit away from the Heavens for the sake of mankind, for the sake of the earth herself. He brought the sun at midnight, light into the darkness, love to Man, the lost son of God. This is the event of Christmas in the history of the world.

At Christmas time we can feel very distinctly how two events are intermingled, the turning point in the earth's life and the coming of Christ, the Son of God, into the world of Man. Thus we say quite naturally: Christmas is happening. It happens in the sun, and on earth. Once, at the turn of world history, it happened in Palestine. It happens again in our midst each year in the Holy Nights. When our feeling penetrates deeper into this happening, we find at the core the mystery of birth. We can contemplate what is born in the life of the earth and what is born for our human life during the holy season.

Let us look first outside the human sphere to the realm of stones, plants and animals. An old legend tells that every Christmas Eve the cows and oxen, the horses and the asses kneel down to worship in their stables, in memory of the ox and ass who stood round the manger of the Child born in Bethlehem. Nowadays, people are only just beginning to realise again that the Christian festivals are shared with the other creatures of the earth. The legend is one of the few reminders that this was more widely recognised in earlier times.

The whole earth is in harmony with the Heavens in the Holy Nights. A great event takes place among the plants. They take their form and character from the stars and planets that move through the sky. At this time they receive the communication of their forms from above in preparation for the coming spring. They are inspired with the pictures of what they shall become. The Heavens send down the guiding thoughts and the soul of all the plant kingdom is open to receive and be filled. There would be neither flower nor fruit in the season to come, if the listening earth would not commune with the Heavens for the sake of the seeds and roots within the ground. From one year to another, seed and bulb, root and stem, pass on the substance of last summer's plant to that of the next. The warmth of last summer's sunshine has entered into the seeds and ripened them. But they cannot grow into new plants without the renewed influence and touch of the stars. The poet Blake spoke of "the eternal image that returns in the seed". Star-born is this image and star-given must it be each year at the turn of midwinter.

The stones and the minerals receive their form and image likewise from the Heavens. They do not flower and fade with the seasons like the plants, but all the year round they rest in the form which they received at their shaping. They contemplate unceasingly the starry sphere of their origin, but during the Holy Nights their contemplations and that of the plants are united. At other seasons the plants are occupied in growing and withering, flowering and fruiting. The animals are heaven-begotten as much

as the plants and stones. Those who hibernate give themselves
entirely to the earth's contemplation of the Heavens. The others
share also in the blessing from the source of their being in the stars.
It is the holy time of consecration, when the life of all the earth's
creatures is quickened at the hand of God.

Many of the well-loved old pictures of the Madonna and
the Child show the ox and the ass at the crib and the shepherds
coming with sheep and dogs. The stable in Bethlehem is often
surrounded with flowers, that have wonderfully come into
blossom in winter to greet the newborn Son of God. Dürer
painted one scene, into which he seems to have put every animal,
bird and plant that he knew and for which he could find its
tiny corner. Such pictures are most complete when angels are
there too beside the plants and beasts, either singing, flying or
adoring the Child. Here the thought of Christmas time comes
to expression. The continuing life and beauty of the earth comes
from her communion with the Heavens.

The picture of the Mother with the Child is the heart of the
Christmas festival. The birth of every child is an event filled with
wonder, because the Heavens are opened each time to let a being
of Spirit enter the world of matter. The newborn babe is in a
spiritually true sense brought by the angels to the parents who
have prepared his body and now take charge of his young life.
The birth of the Christ child carries within it the holiness of all
birth and still transcends it further. Each child is an eternal soul
belonging to the family of Mankind, carrying in himself part of
the whole human destiny. The Christ-being is of a higher order,
not bound by the necessity of His own nature to seek life on the
earth. His cosmic dwelling was the sun. His destiny belonged to
the universe. Nevertheless He took on the form of a man. He
concentrated His divine Being into human shape. He, the Son
of God, sought of His free will, as an act of sacrifice, to become

the Son of Man. He accepted the earthly destiny of mankind as His own and began to transform it.

At the time of Christ's incarnation, Mankind was in the greatest danger. The two worlds of Heaven and Earth had been separating more and more since the Fall of Man began. The being of Man partook of this separation and became increasingly divided. The earthly image of Man was separated from the divine idea which had been created in the World of God at the beginning of time, and was losing its true nature. Then Christ appeared in human form, revealing in Himself the divine pattern which Mankind had lost. The Child that is worshipped at Christmas is the picture of the heavenly idea of Man, sent down in Christ from the heights of Heaven to the depths of earth. Just as the plants receive their divine image during the Holy Nights, so do human souls at Christmas time behold in the Holy Child the pattern for the sake of which they were created. They recognise that Man will find the true humanity designed for him in the mind of God, by the grace of Him who came down to share his earthly existence.

That which is born at Christmas for the whole of Mankind is born at the same time for each human soul. The spiritual essence of the human being, our true self, is brought down into the soul by Christ. There is a spirit-child born within each one of us through His coming. It is the promise of our true, future humanity, of that which we still have to become. Christ in us is a living fact, that we recognise again and worship anew each Christmas time. The mystery of the new birth takes place within each human heart that is inclined towards Christ and that longs to be born anew in His image. The Christ child is the pattern for the divine spiritual being in ourselves. The Son of God has become the Son of Man, that the child may be born within the children of human beings, through whom they shall become the children of God.

Whom do we rever in Mary, the mother of the Holy Child? Many meanings are gathered together in such a universal picture as that the Madonna. She is the single human soul, in whom all the forces of goodness and devotion are gathered to transform the heart in her image. Within each heart, the mother can receive the Holy Child. She is likewise the soul of all Mankind, in the innocence of Man's divine beginnings, receiving the Spirit of Man. The picture can be expanded still further until she appears as the world-soul, begotten of the creative forces of the whole universe. The stars are around her head, the sun clothes her, the moon is under her feet and the blue widths of space are her mantle. She is the Madonna of all time, bearing the man-child from age to age. Today He appears again in the new revelation in the sphere of the clouds. Christmas is never finished, never just the remembrance of something past and done.

Once, the Madonna took on human form. As a young, homeless mother, she sought the place where her child could be born in the stable at Bethlehem. Then she became again the Queen of Heaven among the stars, a sign in the universe from age to age. The Child, who became Man, remains Man, but He is lifted up that all may behold Man as a cosmic being, with a destiny in the universe, with a calling among the starry worlds of Heaven. The cosmic meaning of Christmas transforms it into a festival that continues from age to age, unfolding each time it comes again the spiritual mystery of birth.

THE NATIVITY

Christmas comes down to us in the darkness of midnight. In the stillness and quiet it comes, when the clamour of the day has ceased and the world is holding its breath. Then the candles of the stars light up, the moon's lamp illumines the wide spaces of the dark, and in the magical hours of their shining, that is born which is new and which comes only at one season of the year. Christmas brings the mystery of birth, in which from the world-heights the living force is born that renews existence. Throughout the Holy Nights, from Christmas Eve until January 6th, we can feel the mood of blessing and watch without and within the happening of the mystery.

For the people who recognise Christmas rightly, it is the season of candlelight. The candles burn on the decorated trees, in the windows of houses, in the rooms. They are set alight in the dusk and send their little flames upwards, while the great lights of the stars shine downwards from the Heavens. The Christmas candles are the token for the burning hearts of the people who lighted them. Their longing for the Spirit's light, their love towards God, their seeking for the presence of Christ, burn upwards in flames of prayer out of the darkness of the world.

When the shepherds watched their flocks near Bethlehem on the first Christmas night, the darkness was filled with the bright glow of an angel, the quiet sounded with the tones of his voice. He told of a child that had been born at the turn of the night, who should be the long-awaited bringer of salvation. After his words, the whole dome of the sky was illumined by a multitude of angels, who sang the greeting of the Heavens to the creatures of earth. The shepherds heard their song and understood it to say: "the glory of God in the heights, and peace on earth to men of good will". They perceived in their hearts what the heavenly greeting signified. The revelation of God in the heights of Heaven will be shown to humans and they shall receive on earth the substance of His peace, if they accept it in good will. God is giving a new gift to people on earth, they realised, and he who brings it has already been born. The shepherds were simple folk and in all their ways close to nature. Their eyes and ears were attuned to living things, so that they were never far off from the realm of the angels, who weave and move in the flowing substance of life and light. Quite naturally they, in the silent hours of the darkness, were of all people those who could most readily perceive, in a half state between sleeping and waking, the rush earthwards of the angelic hosts who were the companions of the child on his way to the gate of birth. Their seeing would have had at all times a touch of the visionary about it. Then, for once, on that night they became wholly seers, and they heard the song and saw the shining of the angels face to face. Their hearts were awake, when wakefulness was most required. On behalf of all other people, of those who were quite asleep and oblivious, of those whose eyes and ears had become blind and deaf to the realm of the angels, they were ready to receive the tidings of God's gift to the world of earth. These watchers in the night were the first to know what the angels were proclaiming.

The shepherds took what they heard straight into heart and will. In the first light of the morning they came to Bethlehem, and found the child lying in the manger as the angel had foretold. They worshipped Him in joy as they divined the heavenly source of their human being. In the light around Him, they felt the promise of a new humanity, in which the being of Man should

 59

become transparent for that of God. Their hearts overflowed with rejoicing and they returned to tell their neighbours how they had seen fulfilled on earth what they had heard from the angels.

So it was once upon a time, when the child was born, around whom shone Christ's light, who was to become the vessel for His Spirit. So it happened in a certain town, in a certain year, that is fixed in the calendar of outer events by a decree made by the Romans. Into the field of human history, of earthly facts and events, entered the being of Him who came down from the Heavens at the midnight of time. The new age of Man's life on earth began with His coming. History turned, and into the stream of its downward course came the newborn trend upward, which is the working of Christ in human evolution. The current flows since then in two directions. That which was initiated by the fall of Man into the power of evil continues downwards and onwards to death. That which entered at the turn of time with Him who was sent from above, is set towards the heights and leads on to the Divine World. The source of this current is found in the birth of the Christ child on the first Christmas night.

At Christmas we look up into the sky and watch in the darkness of winter for the renewal of the sun's light. We feel the creatures of the earth listening for the inspiration from the spheres of the stars, who rain down their influences once more to make new all existence below. We look back in time to the midnight of our history, when the light of Christ was born into this world, which had fallen into the dark power of evil and death. His coming is the fact from which our human existence takes new life, and yet many souls are asleep and only a few are awake to recognise what has taken place. Then we look into our own time. Christmas is a mystery renewed every year, a spiritual event happening again and again. The Madonna and the Child are in myself. My soul is woven from the forces of the stars, though they are now caught and held in the confines of my personality. The good and innocent powers of the universe can live in my heart and their strength can transform it into the likeness of the mother who receives the heavenly child. The Spirit enters my soul as the child, who shall be born and grow until my whole being is transformed by the Christ-given grace. The future human being made in His image is within me as the spirit-child, who is born in my heart because He once entered the life of Man on earth. When the plants are inspired from the stars above with the patterns from which they will blossom in the coming spring, they receive something that has been already created and completed in the Heavens. When the future being of Man is born in the human soul, there comes to life that which is not yet known in the universe, which should grow and mature here on earth. The pattern of Man's new divine image is not above but within. It is hidden with Christ in us. The heavenly Child, the Son of God, is the secret of Christmas within ourselves, which we discover again in the holy time.

Those who are awake in heart at this season, who watch in spirit like the shepherds, find the power of insight growing stronger within. They look towards the future and see the path of life opening before them. Very few are the people who dare nowadays to look ahead. "Let us get what we can and enjoy it while it lasts" is a common point of view. The true experience of Christmas, however, brings clearer vision into the future and a braver sense of purpose. Christ has entered the realm of earth. We recognise it in our inner life, we read it in the course of history. He has brought the vision of what is our purpose and calling, of the end which the Kingdom of Heaven wills to achieve in the destiny of mankind. Our minds may awaken at Christmas time to the great ideas towards which those strive who follow Him who revealed the human pattern divine in Himself. Therein lies the inspiration for all times to come. He who came to save Mankind has not taken the struggle from our life on earth, nor the suffering from our great tribulation. But a new sense has been given to human experience. An element of healing is present when earlier only the touch of death was to be felt. The process of salvation has been initiated and continues unceasingly to work within the events of human life. Chaos, destruction and suffering are not in vain. They can be transformed into the soil in which seeds of Spirit may take root. In the past, when human souls looked for the light shining into the darkness of the world, they turned their gaze back to the beginning of creation and up into the Heavens. Since the coming of Christ we likewise behold the radiance of the divine light above in the Heavens and far back at the source of our existence. Then we find it again from a new direction. We look within ourselves and find the light. We look towards the distant end of evolution and find the light sending its beams from the future into the present. The path of life is illumined from the past and from above, from the future and from within. Christmas is the festival of the world's light born into the darkness. The little flames of the Christmas candles are lighted as a sign of our heartfelt devotion to the Light of the World. They burn with the will that is rekindled in the holy season to do the work of the Light, letting its healing power transform the darkness within and without.

EPIPHANY

EPIPHANY

January 6th is by old tradition the day of the Three Kings. The season of the Holy Nights comes to an end and that of Epiphany, which lasts four weeks, begins. The picture of the wise men from the East, following the star until they found the Child, accompanies us all through this period. It is almost more difficult for people with a modern cast of mind to realise the necessity for this custom than that of celebrating Christmas for twelve days. We are a restless generation today, accustomed to getting one thing over quickly in order to pass on to the next. But the Christmas festivals are no more to be hurried than the seasons, which take their own natural time. There is a space of preparation for all the great festivals and one for looking back, for gathering the fruits of experience, for taking what has been received. In such a manner is the season of Epiphany related to Christmas.

The great happening of Christmas is the appearance of the Son of God in human form on earth. The Divine Father is the giver of the revelation, which Mankind receives. Human souls need time and contemplation to make the gift their own. With other great experiences in life it is the same. At the time the impact of the event is too strong for one to realise altogether what it means or to make effective the changes in oneself that it calls forth. This process cannot be passed through at once. If it is hastened, much that might have happened may well be lost. So it is with Christmas. Each time the festival comes round, those who truly celebrate it pass on into the rest of the year as different people. They have a greater, deeper understanding of Christ's coming.

The living force of His presence works in them more strongly. They have become more Christ-inclined, more devoted to the Spirit-child within. Time is needed for the transformation to deepen, for understanding to mature, for the heart to learn to pray with new power. Epiphany is the time in which the gift of Christmas becomes substance in the souls of men.

Outside in the world of Nature the change that was wrought during the Holy Nights is beginning to take effect. The sap has begun to rise in the branches, the seeds have begun to swell. The inspiration from the stars will gradually find expression in leaf and flower. As an artist, who has long cherished in his thought and feeling a certain idea, begins to bring it into shape and to compose it in stone, wood or paint, so the artist Nature has reached the moment in the course of the year when she can prepare to put forth in living substance the ideas she has received from the universe. To outer appearance, the land looks bare, cold and desolate just after Christmas, unless it is clothed with a magic garment of snow. But underneath there is a stirring of life and growth and the cold atmosphere is shot through at intervals with a thrill of quickening power.

The token of Advent was described as the rainbow, that of Christmas the sun. Now in Epiphany it is the star. In Christmas time the Heavens are opened and human hearts are lifted up to behold the radiance of the Spirit-Sun, who is Christ. When the moment of revelation is past, the shadows of earthly existence close round our hearts again. We have to continue day by day along the path of our destiny on earth. We cannot always live in the dawn of enlightenment. Yet we are not bereft of the light.

Like the wise men from the East, who journeyed to find the Child, the way through earthly life is lighted by the star of Christ. In earlier ages the stars had a significance for human beings which at present is largely forgotten. They were the source of divinely inspired wisdom. Nowadays, anyone who wants to know more starts to read books and to study the printed page. Among the ancients, the night sky was looked upon as the great world book. The shining stars were the letters and the constellations were the words. As the stars moved and the planets circled among them, so the script changed. What we read today in books is the wisdom of human minds. What they read in the book of the sky was the wisdom of the gods, of the whole Divine World. It was the revelation of the will of God, by which they ordered and arranged their life and affairs on earth.

The Christmas star has another meaning. The star-filled sky reveals the order and justice of God in the universe. The star of Christ brings the new revelation of grace. Our feeling in the time of Epiphany can be filled with the warmth and glow of this newly given element of grace. It is an expression of the nature and working of Christ and is found in our world of earth only through and from Him. Our single destinies and that of all Mankind are woven from substance of two kinds, from the necessity which follows from the world order and from grace. There are events in the human lifetime which are clearly the result of what has gone before, whether in a happy or an unhappy sense. Other opportunities come to meet us, far more than as a rule we notice, which come from the future and can be used by our free creative power to ends that cannot be foreseen. We are not only creatures driven along by the necessities of our own nature or the results of our doings. We have a source of free activity in our souls, by which we have the capacity to make and shape our lives through the opportunities that come to meet us.

In the order of the universe the moon is the source of all the forces of necessity. Her influence orders and controls divine justice. The sun, on the other hand, has the power to give grace, to penetrate the order of life with undeserved opportunity, with enthusiasm for free activity. Before Christ's coming, divine order and justice was worshipped when the hearts of men and women were lifted to the cosmos of stars by night. At His coming a new star shone, with the warm glow of the sun but in the company of the night-radiant stars. Divine justice is lit up by grace. Since that time, the followers of Christ find the star of grace going before them along the way of salvation that passes through the tribulation of earth.

The star of the Spirit shines into the darkness of the world. The content of thought for this season is the incarnation of Christ, the birth of God among men. An old tradition from the early days of Christianity places in this part of the year the day of remembrance for the baptism in Jordan. It is necessary to the festival of Epiphany that this should be so, because the baptism represents the historical moment when Christ took on the bodily existence of a man on earth. A distinction is to be made between Jesus and Christ. Jesus was the man, Christ the Son of God. The body and soul of Jesus were prepared for thirty years for the event of Christ's birth. One part of the being of Jesus, his human self, withdrew to allow the Spirit of Christ to enter the bodily house which had been made ready. The life of Jesus up to that moment was the most beautiful of all human lives. It was filled with pure devotion to the coming of Christ. The soul of Jesus was profoundly aware of the power of sin and evil, by the helplessness of human souls. His heart was inspired with compassion so great that wherever he went his presence gave warmth and light like the sun. The picture of what a good man can be was never better fulfilled than by Jesus of Nazareth.

At the baptism in Jordan, he consciously sacrificed his own being for Christ. Then the Heavens opened and the voice of the All-Father was heard from above: "This is My beloved Son". Jesus offered himself from the earth to the Heavens.

Christ offered Himself from the Heavens to the earth. Without any necessity out of His own nature, He came down into the darkness of this world to share the tribulation of Mankind. He came to bring the way of salvation to the souls of men. He was sent as the messenger of the sons of God in the Worlds of Spirit, who in divine compassion longed to give healing to the sickened, sinful men and women who had been themselves at the beginning children of God.

There is no contradiction between such an interpretation of the baptism of Jordan at Epiphany and that of the Holy Child at Christmas. The Child is the picture of all that is born into Mankind and into the world of Earth by the coming of Christ. The fact that, historically and humanly speaking, the babe born in Bethlehem to Mary and Joseph was Jesus, the man, does not alter the reality that the Child of Christmas is the Christ child. The story of the wise men from the East is a key to its meaning. The kings were called by the star and they were guided on a long journey to Bethlehem in Palestine. They offered gifts and worship to the One they found at its direction. They saw in the child the greatest, wisest and most self-sacrificing of human souls. The deed of Jesus could be performed only by the most perfect of men. They saw in the star over His head the light of Christ, which was already shining in the earthly world, though not yet from within a human body. At the baptism in Jordan the star and the child became one. The Spirit of Christ entered the world at the first Christmas, when the angels called the shepherds and the star the wise men. He entered the human body, in which He dwelt for three years, when Jesus was baptised and the Heavens opened to send down the dove of the Spirit and the sound of the Divine Father's voice.

The stories from the four Gospels of the life and work of Jesus Christ are the natural content for contemplation in this season.

In order of time, these will come first which tell of the childhood of Jesus, especially that of the meeting with the wise doctors in the temple. Then will follow those that tell of His working, His teaching and His healing. The whole period between Christmas and Easter should be filled with the effort to gain an understanding of the earthly life of Jesus Christ, as it is described in the Gospels. The apparent simplicity of their accounts hides deep mysteries of the Spirit that are not easily penetrated by the way of thinking that is natural to us today. It is wiser to become aware of questions and problems, when reading the Gospels, than to believe in one's own understanding of the words. Respect for their mystery is the beginning of wisdom. Christ came to earth as the messenger from the Heavens. He came to fulfil what the beings of God expected, not what was wished and hoped by earthbound human beings. If we read the Gospels from our own point of view, we miss very easily the world-purposes that were undertaken by Him, who was sent to do the will of God.

The pictures from the Gospels are necessary to us now, because the ideal was fulfilled in Jesus Christ of that which all human beings should become. In His speaking, doing and living, He made real and true here on earth the ideal for the future. He revealed what Man can still become. Therein lies the way of salvation, that the children of humanity change and progress in likeness to the Christ pattern. We are still far off from this fulfilment. The pattern has to be impressed still more deeply into our hearts, to fill us with vision and enthusiasm for what should come. In our own time of history Christ is present to help us towards this purpose. As the history of the world evolves, so the working of Christ changes and continues. Moments of climax are reached from time to time when He is revealed to men and women on earth with especial force and clarity. At each of these recurring moments the revelation fulfils and carries further what has gone before. This present century is such an historical climax, when many people, who may or may not be Christians or even devout souls, will know of His presence out of their own experience. The façade of the ordinary world cracks and the realities that are hidden by it appear. Then it will not be a matter of uncertain faith to believe that He is among us, but of actual vision and certainty. This century is filled with tragedy, but the star is shining in its darkness. The tragedy is the effect of the thoughts and deeds of the past. The star is the radiance of grace proceeding from the divine being of Him who continues to show human souls the way of salvation.

THE PILGRIM KINGS

The season of the Holy Nights ends when the festival of the Three Kings, or Epiphany, begins. Our thoughts turn from the Christmas scene described by St Luke with the angels and shepherds to that of St Matthew. It makes a very different picture in darker colours and less joyful mood. A breath of Paradise breathes through St Luke's story of the Nativity. For a moment the guardians have withdrawn the fiery swords and the gate of Eden has opened again to let through the brightness of the hidden light and the fragrance of the divine presence. The Heavens are as near as the sky and the angels go to and fro overhead as naturally as the flowers grow underfoot. No devil brings trouble on the scene, though he murmurs in the distance through the shouts of the soldiers executing the decree of the Roman governor and in the harsh refusals of the innkeepers. In this Christmas picture we perceive the inner meaning of the good wishes we send to each other at this season. We see beyond the shadows of existence to the light from the Heavens that kindles in our hearts the flames of good will. After the holy time we go out into the shadows again, but we should not lose the vision of Christmas. At this moment we encounter the story of the three wise men. They came to find the child, travelling a long and toilsome road, seeking their way through the darkness, temptation and danger. They found at last the light that shines in the gloom and is not extinguished by the dark forces of evil. They go before us on the path of experience that leads from Christmas into the weeks of wintertime.

The star shining in the east, in the direction from which the dawn comes, told the wise men in their distant lands that a child was born through whom the new age of history would begin. They were persons of great authority in their own world, whose wisdom made them leaders of men. They knew how to read the golden writing that is written in letters of light by the stars as they move over the night sky.

When the descent of the Son of God to earth was prepared in the spheres of the Father, His journey downward was reflected in the constellations. The star that the wise men followed is the picture for His divine Presence when He was entering the sphere of the earth. An old legend relates that when the kings first saw the star, it shone at night with the warmth and glow of the sun. That is a way of saying in a picture that the wise men saw the age of the old wisdom pass into decline and the new one begin to appear. In the radiance of the moon, during the dark watches of the night, people had gathered what they needed to know for the ordering of their life on earth. In the time to come, wisdom would be found in the daylight of consciousness, through the spiritual power of the sun. The wise kings beheld the rising star and understood what it meant. They accepted the passing of the old and set out to find in his earthly form the bearer of the new. Quick and easy as had been the way of the shepherds to Bethlehem under the guidance of the angel, so the journey of the kings was long and difficult. Before they could find the child, they had to enter the realm of the adversary, to meet the powerful King Herod.

The old legend says that the kings travelled far but swiftly until they neared Jerusalem, when they were lost in a fog and could no longer see the guiding star. This incident truly describes the sphere of spiritual darkness round Herod. He was a king but the opposite of the three wise men. He was a ruler by force and fear, without wisdom and justice. He knew only that which his servants read to him from the old book of the prophets. His heart was dark with the dread of losing his power. When he heard of the birth of one who would be by divine right the King of Kings, his only wish was to destroy him whom the wise men wished to worship. They could only reach Bethlehem by first going to Jerusalem, by learning the road from the enemy of the child, by meeting him face to face. Nor had they the discernment to recognise Herod for what he was. An angel came to them later, in a dream, to warn them against returning to his city. When they left Jerusalem behind on the last stage of their journey they looked up and beheld again the star whose guidance they followed until they came to a certain house in Bethlehem.

The kings knelt down before the mother with the child in her arms and worshipped him, offering the gifts of gold, frankincense and myrrh. They recognised one who would bring wisdom greater than theirs, whose kingship would begin where theirs ended. The gifts which they presented were tokens of the three great ages of history that had preceded the coming of Christ. The frankincense spoke of the genius for devotion to the Divine World that inspired the most ancient Indian culture. The souls of humans had lived then in a continuous turning in love and understanding to the spheres of Heaven. The gold was a sign of the spiritually enlightened wisdom that was the glory of the following culture centred in ancient Persia. In that time people learnt to bring the heavenly knowledge down to earth and to transmute its teaching into fruitful work. The myrrh was the token of the ancient culture of Egypt, in which the souls of humans began to find their home in the earthly world and thereby to discover the real presence of evil and death. Myrrh is the substance precious for its use in embalming dead bodies and in healing sickness. As a gift it spoke mutely of the dark knowledge of death that had come to human souls and the longing for the healing of Man's nature from sin. Like ambassadors for the whole of Mankind, like representatives of the earlier ages of human history, the three wise men knelt before the child so newly come from the Heavens and offered the treasure betokening all that this world had to give.

The gifts of the kings were like fruit ripened on plants that have already withered, like corn harvested at the end of the summer from dry, yellow straw. The ages of history in which they had been brought forth were passed, the forces that had formed them were gone. The wise men worshipping the child had finished their pilgrimage. Offering their gifts, they had come to the end of their task and their powers.

Behind the ending of the story, behind the picture of their departure into their distant lands, lies a mystery. The holy child was taken at the angel's behest to Egypt. Then the crowd of little children died by the swords of Herod's soldiers in Bethlehem. The hand of death is stretched out over the final scene and touches the kings who have gone their ways home. The ancient, wonderful past of mankind's history dies in the wise men, and the beautiful childhood of Man dies in the holy innocents who are massacred. Before they died, they have offered what they had to Him who has entered the world of earth from the heights of Heaven. The kings have brought gifts; the children have given their young lives.

When Christmas is behind us, the path of experience lies open towards Easter. The mystery of sacrifice is foreshadowed in the story of the kings. Christ is He who brings life out of death, who transforms the offering of the past into seed for the future. The wise, mature men and the young, innocent children had laid their sacrifice into His hands. They had set their spirit-feet on the road to Easter, following Him through His divine destiny on earth. They were ready to take death and resurrection as their lot, to unite their life with the process through which what they had offered could become seed and bear new fruit within the working of Christ.

Among the stories of the life of Jesus Christ in the Gospels are those describing how the dead are called back to life, the daughter of Jairus, Lazarus, and the widow's son of Nain. Before Christ Himself passed through death and resurrection, He called certain souls back to life on earth. He revived in them forces of Spirit that were dying out of human existence because the souls of humans had become too weak in the struggle with temptation and evil. When the young daughter of Jairus began to live again, when Lazarus came forth from the grave, when the young man of Nain returned to his widowed mother, the soul of Man was healed and quickened, receiving again with fresh strength the qualities that had flowered and borne fruit in the ancient cultures, which had come to maturity and had fallen into decay before Christ's coming.

The three kings had taken gold, frankincense and myrrh to the child in Bethlehem. They had lost their way on their journey, they had gone for guidance to the court of Herod, betaking themselves unknowingly into the stronghold of the adversary. Only the dream of the angel saved them from betraying the child they came to worship. The past history of Mankind is pictured transparently in the simple story of the journey, on which the wise men were led by illusion into error and lost the guidance of the heavenly star. Nevertheless, they kept faith in the one main particular: they brought their gifts to the true king. They did not mistake Herod for Him whom they sought. The star found them again and they made the offering rightly. Because of what they offered, Jesus Christ was able at a later time to raise again in the dead whom He called to life the forces of Spirit from which had grown the fruits of human existence represented in gold, frankincense and myrrh. Had Christ not come, had the kings not brought their gifts, had they not found the star again that showed them the right way, the fruits of Mankind's endeavour in the great ages before the turn of time would have been lost. They are coming to life again in the souls of men, they will blossom yet more in times not yet come, because in the hands of Christ the new seed has quickened and sprouted from the old, withering husk.

Each year at Christmas time we look back to the beginning of the way of salvation. Understanding of what our present life means grows in our hearts through what we have seen. Man's history since the coming of Christ appears as the long road of salvation stretching away into the distant future and ourselves as pilgrims upon it. Our present life is part of a long pilgrimage which we make in company with every other human soul in whom shines the true purpose of being human. Every day in each lifetime is a step forward, a standing still, or a step astray from the straight path. The way is long and full of effort. The end is in the distance and at times is hard to see distinctly. The temptation is always near to sit down and pause by the roadside, to become an onlooker at the march of life. The road of salvation is trod with courage and a clear sense of purpose. Over it shines the star of Christ, pointing the way, sending the grace of warmth and enlightenment into human hearts. Strength and courage flow into us when we look up to see the star, calling us, as it once called the three wise men, to follow its guiding light.

BETWEEN CHRISTMAS AND EASTER

INCARNATION AND TEMPTATION

The sun shines down from the sky, shedding from his beams warmth, light and life from above upon the earth below. When we look at the sun we behold the golden heart of the universe and we can feel beating within our breasts the little heart that is an image of the great one in the Heavens. The inner, spiritual virtue of the sun is faithfully expressed in the outer appearance. In ancient times the Sun-spirit was often worshipped as the greatest among the gods. Those who prayed to Him were in fact sending their prayers to Christ, in the existence which He had before He incarnated on earth. The outer form of the sun in the sky is a picture for the inner nature of Christ. We may say of Him: He is the sun. Once upon a time this was true in a different sense. Then the sun was not His picture but the temple in which He dwelt, from which He performed His office in the order of the universe. When He came down to earth, His spiritual Being vacated the heavenly dwelling and entered the house of a human body.

How could such a change in the existence of a divine Being come about? Very long preparations were made to produce a body fitted to be His habitation. When Abraham was separated from his folk in order to found a tribe of his own, this was the mission destined for his descendants. The god Jehovah led this people through the course of their history and gave them laws by which they lived. One purpose inspired all their experiences and the manner of their life, to bring forth the kind of human body in which a god could dwell on earth. Many generations were numbered before the sons of Abraham had so refined and perfected their forces of heredity that Joseph and Mary could become the parents of the child who was born in Bethlehem. The table of His ancestors, which is given in the first verses of St Matthew's Gospel, bears witness to the long, divinely-planned history of the tribe, which prepared for His birth. Each father and mother who made a new link in the chain were touched by the guiding hand of their God. They felt themselves part of a chosen people, elected to help in the fulfilment of a task in which no other race could share. A token of their election was given to keep them in constant remembrance of their mission. Solomon built the Temple according to the plan made known by Jehovah and it became the place of worship for the whole people. The proportions in which it was erected had a secret, inner relation to those on which the perfected temple of the body would be built. Not in outer appearance, but by signs that spoke to the deepest understanding of the heart, the Temple in Jerusalem warned the Children of Israel never to forget the purpose for which they had been chosen.

Every soul, who comes into this world of earth through the gate of birth, enters a body, which has been in the process of being built for a long time. When the body was made ready for the God, who was to dwell in the shape of a man, a still longer preparation was required. His divine Spirit could not enter the form of the newborn child directly. Another being of the human order had first to form and shape the soul and the body until they were fit to receive Him. The most spiritual and mature among human personalities, he who is called in the Gospels Jesus of Nazareth, made ready the house of flesh and the garment of soul to be offered to the Spirit of Christ. The babe born in the stable, the boy who sat among the learned men in Jerusalem, were preparing the vessel which was to be filled later when the young man reached the age of thirty. When that time came, Christ was born into the being of Jesus at the baptism in Jordan.

During the three years that followed until the death on the cross, Christ Jesus lived on earth, the Spirit of God's Son dwelling in the soul and body of a man. The incarnation is a mystery, which succeeding generations of people have striven to understand since it became a fact of history. At some periods men's minds have seen the divine Spirit more distinctly than the human vessel. At others, especially since the Reformation took place, their understanding has more readily grasped the man than the God who took up abode within him. The truth lies in perceiving that the God and the man became one by a process of incarnation that began when John baptised Jesus and continued until it ended in death. God in Man, and Man in God, was He who lived, that once only, in a human body on earth, in order to bring the salvation sent down from the Divine World at the turn of time.

John the Baptist, the prophet in the wilderness, to whom all the people of Jerusalem listened, was the man called upon to do the work of God and help the Spirit of Christ to enter the being of Jesus. He was the herald who prepared the way for His coming. The people who flocked to hear him preach would willingly have taken him to be the Messiah in person. Expectation beat very high at the time, but those who waited for the promised Deliverer expected one who would fit into the accepted pattern of a great leader. John knew that this was not so and gave a negative answer to their questions. He described himself as the voice warning his hearers to prepare for the coming of the true Messiah. He urged them to make themselves ready by a change of heart and conduct. He not only preached but he performed a rite of purification, in which his followers were inwardly changed and awakened to clear consciousness of the crisis in history that was at hand. Many came to him on the banks of the Jordan and were baptised by him in the river. During this ceremony, the past existence of Mankind, the descent from Heaven into darkness and death and the desperate necessity for a means of salvation were revealed to them. They received the most overwhelming experience of a lifetime. John's words no longer came to them from without. They knew from within of what he spoke when he preached.

This same rite of baptism, which John performed on his followers to prepare them to recognise and receive Him who was to come, became the earthly means by which the Spirit of Christ was born into the body of Jesus. John, a man, representing in that hour all Mankind, performed with human hands the act through which the God could descend into existence as a man. Jesus, the youth who had lived entirely in devotion to that for which he had been prepared for thirty years, gave up the sheaths of body and soul to the One greater than he. The living temple had been built. He had been its guardian and its priest until the hour came when the God Himself required it for His dwelling. Jesus withdrew in the process of the shock brought about by the baptism with water. Christ for whom the temple had been built through the long generations since Abraham, entered the human soul and the body of flesh to live therein until Golgotha. The world-creating Logos returned to the creation from which He had withdrawn at Man's fall into sin. The Creator took on the likeness of the creature, that He might bring deliverance to the lost ones, who were so much under the spell of darkness that they did not know Him when He came.

The first experience of Christ in His earthly life is described in the first three Gospels in the scene of the Temptation. It is the token for the whole three years of the incarnation. He met the powers of evil face to face in the wilderness, which is the place of death. It is impossible to imagine that this was a single event which passed and was over. It underlies all that followed in the further events and experiences of the life of Jesus Christ. Looking from the heavenly heights above down on the dark existence of the earth in the state of separation from the divine universe, the Son of God had seen the presence of death from without. Now He stood within it, meeting for the first time this strange state of God-forsakenness. As long as He walked in human form, even in the pleasant land of Galilee, the death that underlies earth-existence was apparent to Him. The powers of evil met Him at the threshold of His earthly life and they accompanied Him all the way until the end. What is openly declared in the scene of the Temptation was present in every scene that followed.

Three requests were made to Him by the devil in the wilderness. In the order described by St Matthew, the first was the temptation to turn stones into bread. The needs of a fleshly body were unknown to the Spirit of Him who had entered the being of Jesus, until in the desert He became acquainted with hunger. Material needs exert power over the souls of men and women and out of this reality the devil conjured the first temptation. The second came from the opposite direction. He was asked to throw Himself down from the pinnacle of the Temple. He was tempted to call on the cosmic powers at His command to overcome the limitations of the body, to lift it magically above the level of matter, at which it is subject to gravity. Having, in the first request, been challenged to take the realm of material substance into His power, in the second He was asked to ignore it completely and overthrow its force with the strength of His cosmic life. Two kingdoms were offered to Him in which to reign, the realm of death where matter truly exists, and the realm of life, which holds the balance with death in earth-existence. In the third temptation, all the kingdoms of the world were put at His command, all the realms of the soul to be experienced in this world, in return for worship and allegiance to be offered to the devil. The powers of evil met Christ at the threshold of earthly life and asked Him to share all they had, if He would work with them and accept their ways in the world.

It was as if they would say: leave us to pursue our ancient ends in the place where the divine order does not hinder us and we will share with You all that we claim as ours. They asked Him to make a third with them, but He replied to them out of the Spirit of the Father-god in the Heavens. He became the third power, not in their sense but in His own. He put His strength between theirs, to hold the balance against them in both directions.

The Gospels speak of the devil meeting Jesus in the wilderness. They do not at first sight seem to distinguish one of the Princes of Evil from the other. The inner nature of the scene, however, discloses the distinction as an open secret behind the general term. Each temptation has a certain direction in space. The request to turn stones into bread looks down into the depths of matter. The second temptation leads into the heights for which the pinnacle of the Temple is a token. The third temptation indicates the widths of space spreading outwards, to left and right. All the kingdoms of illusion, the unreal worlds fabricated out of wishful thinking, woven out of unresolved fears, are offered to the Son of God by the devil, who draws souls to himself through their passionate hopes and dread of earthly realities. In these three directions of space, the mystery of the double nature of evil is both hidden and revealed.

The three directions, towards which the three temptations point, make up the shape of the cross. At the threshold of earthly existence, Christ met in an experience of the soul the cross on which, at the end, His body was to hang. Throughout the time He walked on earth, He was carrying the cross. He knew what lay at the end of the road, but when He endeavoured again and again to tell his followers, they could not understand. They were not able to look at the cross He carried while He was with them, nor at the one set up on the hill of Golgotha, towards which the way led. Human imagination is so limited that it is hard even in contemplation to realise how great was the suffering of earth-existence for Christ and how great was the strength of Spirit necessary to enable Him to fulfil His work.

When the Son of God dwelt in the body of a man, He could not enter the strange dwelling at once. Gradually, through all the three years of His existence in the shape of Jesus, the Spirit of Christ was penetrating stage by stage further into incarnation in the body. At the same time the body was changing under the force of the divine Spirit dwelling within it. Right into the skeleton of bone entered the spiritualising effect. There was a danger that the intense spiritual life within would dissolve away the whole frame before the hour of Golgotha was reached. Christ was engaged in a continual struggle to keep the body of Jesus whole and to remain within it until He would no longer need incarnated existence. The will to work on earth, with which He descended from the heights of Heaven into the narrow limit of the human form, was directed throughout the time of the incarnation to keeping His hold upon flesh and blood, against their natural tendency to dissolve in the fire of His Spirit.

The scene of the Temptation stands at the opening of His earthly life, indicating its whole character. At the close, the same theme returns in another scene which took place in the Garden of Gethsemane. The suffering that is only hinted at in other parts of the Gospels is disclosed here, but not because it was felt only in that hour. The climax was reached then of that which had been the experience of Christ since He entered first the body of Jesus. The very nature of earthly existence, the pressure of flesh and blood upon the Spirit, were the source of this suffering. It is out of the question that the agony in the garden came from fear of losing the body in death. It was just the opposite. How, after the long struggle to maintain bodily existence, could the Spirit find strength for the final trial of the cross and the fight with the real force of death below the surface of earthly life? How could a premature release from the bodily state, an immediate return to the many mansions of the Heavens, be hindered? The Spirit was, in fact, strong enough not to let go the body before the deed was accomplished on Golgotha. Christ did not refuse the bitter cup of earthly existence.

The incarnation ended on the cross, but not the abiding presence of Christ in the realm of earth. He will never a second time inhabit a body of flesh and blood, for all that He could, by so doing, accomplish is already done. Since Golgotha the earth herself has become the dwelling place of His Spirit. The God who reigned once upon the sun abides with the earth until the end of her time. The incarnation was one means of being present in the world. After it was over, His presence endures through times to come but in the state of spirit. The sun has given his spiritual being to the earth. She guards her treasure until the course of her destiny is complete.

THE BEATITUDES

The Sermon on the Mount is the first piece of Christ's teaching recorded in the Gospel of St Matthew. We read there that He gathered the apostles together and sat down with them in a high place. Then He gave them the first instruction in Christianity. The multitudes of people who flocked round Him where He went did not share this experience. Only the twelve who walked with Him day by day were His hearers. On other occasions, in later passages from the Gospels, the same distinction is to be found. The inner circle was told what the crowds could not understand. The multitudes heard parables and pictures, while the apostles received clear thoughts, expressed in pictorial language. Yet careful reading of the Gospels shows that the chosen twelve were told what they heard for the sake of the others, who listened only to the parables. Jesus Christ gave His teaching for all human souls, for the enlightenment of everyone who can hear and understand. Nevertheless, He made a distinction between people with varying states of mind and consciousness. These who were ready to grasp clear thoughts were different for the time being from those who still lived in a mental world of impressions and pictures, felt rather than thought.

If a number of people take a country walk together, it is natural that those go on ahead who know the way. No one who is uncertain about the destination will object to following those who know where it lies. Similarly, the apostles were prepared by their Teacher to be those who most clearly foresaw the aim and end of Mankind's path of evolution, in the new, Christian sense. They were so taught that they might become the guides of the others, who could see less clearly for a while, but who had every chance of learning to share the vision of those whom they followed. The apostles were not intended to form an inner circle equipped with knowledge that was kept from those outside. Such a chosen few would have been brought into the temptation to use secret wisdom for power over the masses. They received the Christian teaching first, that they might be prepared to show the way towards salvation to others. They were instructed in the purposes and aims which Christ brought into the destiny of Man on earth.

The Beatitudes, with which the Sermon on the Mount opens, show in themselves what was the character and intention of Christ's teaching. So much is concentrated into the compass of these few sentences that they may well serve as a pattern for all those passages in the Gospels in which He proclaimed His revelation in words. Nine statements, each beginning with the word "blessed", are their content. The last of the nine is slightly different in style from the others. Instead of "blessed are they", it begins "blessed are ye when". Some readers of the Bible omit it from the series and reckon the Beatitudes to be only eight. In this context they will be treated as nine. Each sentence is compiled in the same manner, with a striking contrast between the first word "blessed", which is repeated each time, and the phrase "in themselves" which begins the second half. The Authorised Version of the English Bible somewhat obscures the stress that should be laid upon these two expressions. The true sense in modern speech of the word "blessed" would be "God-filled". Such a rendering lifts the imagination up towards the Heavens, of which the very substance is the presence of God and paints in the mind a picture of the divine fullness, outpoured and overflowing into the hearts of men. This world of earth in which we dwell is not filled with the being of God. It is the work He has finished, on which His creative mind has been impressed, but from which He has withdrawn. The fullness of His presence is in the Heavens, yet, through the coming of Christ, human souls will partake of the Divine, will receive the substance of the Spirit into themselves. To be blessed is to find the kingdom of God dwelling within the soul. As a plant opens and flowers in the light and warmth of the sun, so the soul expands and fills with radiance when the divine light shines within.

These in whom the conditions of being "God-filled" are present find, so say the nine sentences, the kingdom of God "within themselves". When these words were first spoken to the apostles, they brought about a new beginning in the history of Mankind. In the distance of the future a new aim and end appeared, towards which the souls of the Twelve gazed in uncomprehending wonder. What was this human soul, that the kingdom of Heaven should come to dwell within? Those who had until that time called upon God in prayer looked, not within, but up into the heights of the universe and sought Him there. Old capacities of the soul had long survived, and were only then in process of being finally extinguished, which enabled people, while still alive on earth, to perceive something of the life in the spheres of the Heavens. People had in all the ages of their history looked outwards and upwards to the Divine. Now the apostles heard the nine-times-repeated "in themselves they shall find". The whole direction of their spiritual life had to be changed.

Christ brought about the greatest revolution in the nature of humanity that had been since the world began. Through the work of the two princes of evil, Lucifer and Ahriman, human souls had, before His coming, acquired a sense of self and the power to assert their self-will. What they had so developed in themselves had the effect of cutting them off more and more from the kingdom of God in the Heavens. The dark and sinful character of selfhood was known and no release was found from the disintegrating effects of the state into which Mankind had fallen. He who came from the Heavens brought a new reality of Spirit to be implanted into the sick human souls. He gave to them the spiritual quality of selfhood. He planted the seed of the true self, the grain of actual godhood, into the individual hearts of men. The spiritual virtue of the higher ego began to be present, that the fruits of self-will might become self-sacrifice and self-responsibility. Human nature from that time on should be created again in a new pattern, by a process of growth that should commence from within. The Beatitudes give knowledge of the second birth of Man that is to be fulfilled through the power of Christ. They set forth in nine aspects the new picture of Man, into which the individual souls are to be transformed when they are "God-filled", finding "in themselves" the power of the Spirit.

The portrait of the new Christian human being is drawn in the Beatitudes. To be redeemed, Man will have to be changed and re-made in his whole nature. The future human beings who follow the Christian pattern will become a new race so different from what we are now, that we can hardly imagine them. The Son of God came to seek and save men, but the work of salvation involves the most thorough transformation in soul and in body. He has not undertaken to save people as they are, nor to make them into examples of what they would like to be. At the outset of His mission on earth, He described in the Sermon on the Mount how completely the being of man is to be remodelled in all its parts and what qualities are to be cultivated in human souls to make them fit for the process of redemption. He came to save by making all things new within human nature through the power of the indwelling Spirit.

The first sentence of the nine says that they shall become "God-filled" who become beggars for the Spirit: in themselves shall they find the kingdom of God. Before the soul can beg for the Spirit, the consciousness must have awakened that the human being, here on earth, is separated from the Divine World. In the depths of every heart this is known to be so, but an effort of mind is required to make it conscious. All of us have been through the experience of birth, though we may seem to have forgotten it. We have lived before we were born in the spheres of the Heavens and shared the existence of spiritual beings. Then we have felt the pull earthward and have been aware of the growth of a body, towards which our eternal soul was being attracted. We have passed through the crisis of the body's birth into independent life and have known that the soul was dismissed in that hour from the realms of the Spiritual World. Entering the physical body, we have been separated from the kingdom of God, where we once dwelt. This memory may be deeply hidden in the unconscious; it is nevertheless present in us all. It comes to our notice when we feel the impulse to pray. A natural capacity for prayer lives in every human heart. It may be left to lie unused in the dark but it is there and may rise up in moments of desperation. Like all our capacities, it is formed from something that we have learnt and forgotten. One learns a skill by having tried hard to acquire it and then having allowed what one learnt to drop into the unconscious. It returns again to the surface as a capacity. We have forgotten the experience of coming down into the body and feeling ourselves separated from the worlds of Spirit. It returns to us in the impulse to reach out to that from which we are cut off, to turn to God in prayer.

If the ability to pray is brought to light in the soul and is cultivated with understanding, we become beggars for the Spirit. When Christ came to live in an earthly body, He likewise learnt the experience of separation from the Father. Thereupon He did what none of the Sons of God could learn to do in the spheres of the Heavens, He prayed and He taught to those who followed Him the true manner of prayer. He showed how human souls may become beggars for the Spirit. Those who follow Him will find the answer to prayer in themselves. They will discover the presence of the Spirit that dwells within.

God-filled are those that suffer, for in themselves they will find the power of the Spirit to comfort: so runs the second of the Beatitudes. When we enter earthly life, we meet the experience of suffering. We can try to avoid it, since pain is naturally distasteful, but then we never come to grips with reality. We can go to the other extreme and extol pain as good, making it an end in itself. Neither will lead to blessing. God-filled are those who are awakened in suffering to the presence of the Spirit within the soul and who find therein the power to transmute it. Christ showed in His life on earth the example. Dwelling in a human body, with its material weight of flesh and hard, resisting skeleton, was continual suffering for His nature, that was wholly of the Spirit. He bore the pains of incarnation from day to day through His life on earth, until they culminated in the passion and crucifixion. He endured suffering so great that He was in constant danger of being unable to prolong His existence in the body until the appointed hour of Golgotha. His Spirit manifested itself in the power, not to reject suffering nor be lamed thereby, but to overcome and transmute its force into living spiritual strength. From His example, we may learn that this Beatitude can be fulfilled through the quality of creative patience. The Spirit is related to Eternity, life in the body to time. Since His coming, a spiritual force from the sphere of Eternity dwells within our temporal nature. Therein shall we find the source of patience, which transcends dull endurance. Because suffering belongs to the stream of time, that in us which is eternal can so master it, that from it may be born the spiritual power of life. The Spirit that dwells within shall bring comfort.

God-filled are the tranquil, for in themselves they shall inherit the earth. The third Beatitude speaks of that part of human nature where calm and tranquillity have to be established by inner effort. Everyone who looks into his own soul finds that he has to struggle with himself to bring about order and harmony. The state of tranquillity is not passive, a pleasant sleep of the soul. It is an active, wakeful state, in which all forces are concentrated and alert, instead of being dissipated in a confusion of wants, fears and interests. When someone has such command over the powers of his nature, he is capable of acting out of the Spirit that dwells within. Again, the greatest example of such tranquillity is to be found in Jesus Christ, as we read of Him in the Gospels. The forces over which He held control were not only those of a human nature. To Him belonged the cosmic powers of creation that He had wielded at the beginning in unison with the Father-god. He was only able so to walk on earth that the life of those around Him remained undisturbed, that they were free not to recognise Him unless the spiritual eye of faith became seeing within them, by an exercise of tranquillity far beyond our imagination to conceive. The restraint of His powers made possible the work which He came to fulfil. He was the sower, planting the seeds of salvation in earthly life. Each piece of teaching, each of His acts, initiated one part of the new creation of Man and of the world. He came to begin the Christian age of evolution, which shall be fulfilled at the end of time. Those human souls who are strong in tranquillity are able to partake in the process of redemption, that is to say to inherit the earth. They will carry the power of the Spirit into creative action.

God-filled are those who hunger and thirst after the Spirit, for they shall find it in themselves. The soul hungers for that which it lacks, just as the body hungers for refreshment. The body cannot supply its own needs but depends on what is received from the world beyond itself. Just as little is the soul self-sufficient. The Spirit gives life and refreshment from the Heavens in answer to the soul's longing. The soul is not filled with goodness of itself, neither will it receive strength from the life of the world around. Goodness is the fruit brought forth by the Spirit active in the world within. Christ answered this hunger and thirst with the food of His teaching. In the parables He described pictures taken from the existence on earth. He showed to His listeners experiences from daily affairs, a field in which weeds grew among the corn, a fisherman's net with a mixed catch of good and bad fish, labourers hired to work in a vineyard. He made the scenes spiritually transparent, making clear their inner meaning. It was as if He would say: here in earthly life is spiritual and moral wisdom hidden in ordinary experience. Open your hearts to receive the food of the soul, as you take food and drink into your bodies. Wonder is the quality that opens the inner eye to see where wisdom is to be gathered. It is natural to wish for understanding but it is unwise ever to believe that one has achieved it. Those shall be filled with the Spirit who are willing to continue in hunger and thirst, not those who are afraid of longing and want to live in a state of being satisfied. Wonder means continually reaching out to what has not yet been understood and inwardly realised. It is therefore the quality through which we draw near to this Beatitude.

God-filled are those who give love, for in themselves they shall receive love. In the previous sentence the soul reached out to the world beyond itself. Now it turns to other human beings around and finds the inner strength to give to them out of the Spirit within. Many acts of compassion are recorded in the Gospels of Jesus Christ. He gave spiritual food to hungry souls, He healed the diseased and the insane. He gave in a new way, not simply taking hunger, pain and delusion away from those who were healed, but calling to life in themselves the power to overcome the sickness. How often do we read: "thy faith hath saved thee".

What does it mean that in His presence the weak and sick souls were able to put forth the spiritual strength of faith? He gave healing in such a manner that those who received were not people accepting benefits, but ones who had something to give back. They received from Him the true compassion, which quickened the life of the Spirit in their own hearts. It is easy to confuse pity with compassion, but pity is bounty which is so given by the stronger one that the weaker can do nothing but accept or reject. Compassion means "feeling with", sharing the warmth of the heart with one's neighbours in such a manner that they can give freely in return. It is the quality of feeling out of which we can strive for the grace to give mercy and to receive it.

God-filled are the pure in heart, for in themselves they shall see the presence of God. Christ has given to human souls an essence of the Spirit in the higher self, who has come to dwell within the heart. We have become temples for spiritual beings who are really present within, though they remain hidden unless we seek them. When we say "I", we may speak with the ordinary, self-seeking ego, who comes more obviously to our notice. Nevertheless, we are capable, in moments when the lower self is overcome, of saying "I" out of the true, spiritual self, that is born of the forces of Christ working in us. The heart will have to be first purified of the instincts of the lower self, before it can show forth the God within. In the Gospel of St John Christ described Himself in seven pictures beginning with the words "I am". The Self in Him, which could beget the true self in us, is revealed in these sayings. When we enter into these pictures, we have a glimpse of what selfhood should be in truth. In our own hearts we catch the voice of the Christ-given self in that which is said by our conscience. It speaks to us of the Good, of the ideal from which we fall short, of that towards which we strive. It is the force by which we continue to struggle for purity of heart.

The last three Beatitudes are more difficult of approach, because they speak of that which has not yet appeared within the human soul today. A part of our being is still beyond us, hidden in the world of God, waiting to descend and be realised in our existence on earth. In Christ this spiritual reality has already descended and He continues so to care for the future of Mankind that human souls have not lost the opportunity of receiving, in times to come, the unborn part of their being. The last three Beatitudes are a prophecy, but in Christ they have been already fulfilled. God-filled are the peacemakers. Peace is the substance of the Heavens brought down to dwell on earth. He who came from above brought it with Him as God's new gift to man. Through the crucifixion and the resurrection He united Himself with the being of the earth and began to share the burden of Mankind's evolution. Since that time His Spirit is always present until the end. Where He dwells, lives true, abiding peace. It streams from Him into the hearts of those who can receive it in good will.

The Beatitudes continue: God-filled are they who are persecuted for the sake of the Spirit. They end: God-filled are you, when you are reviled and persecuted. A dark shadow has fallen on these last sentences, as the shadow of men's hate of the Spirit fell on Jesus Christ, so that they put Him to death. Behind the outer aspect of darkness there is an inner one of light. Christ accepted the persecution and performed by its means the deed through which He overcame death. With the strength of the Spirit's life He rose again. With the power of the Spirit, He fashioned the body of the resurrection. He showed, in this risen nature, what the transmuted spirit-created form of Man would be. His resurrection has become the pattern for our resurrection at the end of the world. The true meaning of the last Beatitudes is realised in the Risen One, in whom is made known the ideal towards which we shall strive through times to come.

That which Christ taught, He brought to fulfilment in Himself. What we see in His picture is described and explained in His teaching. This is clearly to be traced in the Beatitudes and it will be found true of all that is recorded of His sayings in the Gospels. He came to teach human beings how to become truly human, and he made real in Himself the pattern which He showed to them. Humans will learn to become truly human when they grow into the image of Him who came from the Heavens to bring the Spirit to earth.

THE HEALING OF THE BLIND MAN

The people who met Jesus Christ in the three years during which He walked on earth found it difficult to recognise Him for what He was in truth. So different were the minds of men and women in those days from what they are now, that the hindrance which prevented them is the opposite from that which holds modern people back from realising the spiritual reality of His presence. They were then so spiritually-minded, so aware that the Heavens were filled with divine beings, whose dwelling-places were the stars, that they could understand Christ as the god of the sun but they could not perceive Him in the simple form of a man. They were so accustomed to worshipping the splendid sun's divinity, to beholding the spiritual radiance of his light, that they could hardly realise that his divine genius had withdrawn from the shining Heavens and actually entered the shades of the earth. Today our inability to grasp the real existence of divine beings hampers our understanding, but at that time the glory of the heavenly company blinded people's perception of what was happening near at hand.

To have insight into the true nature of Jesus Christ was made the more difficult because He did not show on earth the glory He had in the Heavens. He placed under restraint the cosmic power that emanated from His being in the universe. Christ accepted the narrow confines of the body prepared by Jesus. Had He not done so, His appearance on earth would have caused an upheaval in the order of this world so tremendous that its immediate dissolution would have been inevitable. He held His divine power in restraint and veiled the glory, which the people expected to behold, who met Him, hoping for the Messiah. Their state of consciousness, which enabled them to be aware of the divine company filling the Heavens above, made it harder for them to pierce the humble disguise in which Jesus Christ appeared.

The acts of healing described in the Gospels do not contradict such a conception. They are neither a demonstration of superhuman faculties nor a magical means of taking pain, sickness and death away from Mankind. Christ came with the purpose of opening the way to salvation, of initiating the process of redemption through which the Spirit dwelling within human souls shall heal sickness and take the sting from death. He brought the germ of new life to Humanity and His care was to plant and tend it, that people might be able, through Him, to grow and evolve into the new state of redemption. Through the acts of healing He planted seeds which should quicken and bear fruit in the whole human race. Everyone whose disease was cured became in that hour more than themselves. They were made into a representative of Humanity. Their illness was part of the whole sickness of sin with which Humanity was diseased. They were healed not for themselves alone but for the sake of all their fellow human beings, through forces which, working in them, then entered the stream of human evolution to be an abiding source of healing in the sense of Christ.

In the first part of human history that preceded His coming, the healing of sickness came about in another way from that which should be developed since that time. The temples were the places to which the sick resorted and the priests were the healers. The methods of treatment they practised had, in all their variety, the same intention. The souls were to be released for a period from their bodies, to which end a state of sleep was induced. They were brought into the spheres of the universe, where flow the forces of life through which the world was created at the beginning. They were taken, without will or effort of their own, on a journey to the fountain of life, where they could drink a health-giving, quickening draught from the heavenly wellspring of youth. On waking again, the souls returned to the earth renewed by the world's life, harmonised by the influences of the ordered stars, bringing down their new health into the sickened bodies they had left behind. Such was, in essence, the process of healing before the time of Christ. The souls of men and women were taken for a short interval, out of this world where they were a prey to disease and death, into the spheres of deathless life, from which they were cut off on earth by the fall of Man into evil.

When Christ healed the sick a process of another kind took place. What then began has still to be fulfilled in times to come. The earlier method has died out today except for a few last remnants, but the Christian art of healing has not yet grown from the seeds, that were sown in the lifetime of Jesus Christ, to its full revelation. The descriptions in the Gospels of how the sick, the crippled and the lunatics were made whole are prophetic visions of what Christian medicine has still to become. These passages tell quite exactly what manner of healing was initiated by Christ. One, which gives clear illustration to this theme, is the ninth chapter of St John, wherein we read of the man born blind receiving his sight.

The story opens with the question asked of Jesus by the disciples about the cause of the man's affliction. Are his parents at fault: is he suffering from a decadent heredity? Is he himself at fault: is he incapable of taking hold of the body and of developing all his faculties? The answer is given that neither are to blame but that out of this affliction something will be brought forth for the future. This man's blindness is a token for the decadence that had befallen the whole human race at that time. The power of evil increasing from age to age since the separation of this world from the Heavens had first begun, had darkened the eyes of men's souls for the World of God. The inner force of the soul had become so weak in this man that he was no longer able to face the world around him. The spark of divinity in his being, the God within, was imprisoned, separated from the spheres of the Spirit and unable to manifest himself in the life on earth. He expresses the dilemma of Mankind which Christ alone was able to solve. The element of godhood in the human soul on earth had become lost, blind and powerless. Because this man truly represented the state into which Humanity had fallen, he had become blind, helpless and a beggar. His spiritual state had impressed itself on the body.

After this opening we read how the blind man was healed. The story has three parts, the first of which tells how the blindness of his bodily eyes was cured. Then follow the scenes in which he was healed in soul, and lastly comes the picture of his meeting with Christ when sight is given to his inner, spiritual eyes. In a threefold process of healing the entire man was made new and whole. The means by which this came about are described in detail. A number of different forces were concentrated together and their influences were gathered and ordered by Christ, to effect the complete transformation of the poor blind beggar. The miserable specimen of Humanity was changed into an upright, valiant man.

The first element in the process of healing came from the inner being of Christ Himself. "As long as I am in the world, I am the light of the world". So He spoke, who was the Spirit of the sun, come from the heights of Heaven to the depths of earth. Yet He worked differently here below from the sun above pouring out his beams in the spaces of the universe. No one could mistake the sun for what he is, the giver of light and life. If Christ had appeared on earth with the same glorious emanation, everyone would have recognised and worshipped the Son of God. The spiritual essence of the world's light dwelt within Him, enshrined in the vessel of His self, concentrated in that part of His Being from which He spoke, "I am". In this manner it was hidden from the sight of those around Him, unless they had spiritual vision. It was held within the control of His will, to be unloosed by His resolve, never to shine of its own force to dazzle or overwhelm his followers. Christ bore the world's light within the power of His freedom, to give or to withhold, to hide or to reveal. Thereby He gave to people their own freedom. As He carried the Spirit's light in the vessel of His self, so He wished human souls to guard within them a like vessel, enshrining a little flame of divine reality. He came, not to release people from without, but to entrust them with that, to carry within themselves, which He bore within Himself. With this purpose He stood before the blind man, ready to give him on behalf of all humanity the grace to attain salvation, and said: in My power of the I is the world's light.

The healing process began in this manner. The healer stooped down, spat on the ground, and made a clay which He put on the blind eyes. He took some of the soil from the ground. Certain forces of life are still hidden in the earth from the time of creation. Substances in which they live can become medicines, but not until they have been worked upon and changed by human forces. Christ mixed the juice of His own body with that which He took from the earth. At this point the cure was still unfinished. He instructed the blind man to be active himself. He was blind and incapable of living except by begging from other people but he had the use of his limbs to walk. He was told to do something of which he was still capable and, in the telling, he was required to use his faculty of listening and understanding. Another more mysterious force of healing was called into play in what he had to do next. He was not to forget the name of the pool, Siloa, and he may well have repeated it many times to himself, in whispers or aloud. Such ancient sacred names contained the healing power that lives in language. Reciting vowels and consonants that are harmoniously composed into words can still the emotions and calm the forces of the soul. By the time the blind man arrived at the pool, the magic of the name would have brought him into an inner state of harmony helpful to the process of healing.

Another element was present, though it is only mentioned by implication in the story. The helpless man might well have to ask other people to put him on the way to the pool, or perhaps to guide him there. As a beggar he had been dependent on others, now they could help him to be cured. His sickness involved him in a relationship to the other people of his community. They were called on to take part in the healing process. So he came to the sacred pool, of which the water was more than commonly gifted with life-giving powers. The medicine from the element of water was added to that from the earth. He washed, purifying himself inwardly and outwardly of the sickness of sin. Then he came seeing, cured of the blindness of his bodily eyes.

The healing forces of different kinds, that are described in the process by which this man received his sight, are all part of the method of healing initiated by Christ, in contrast to that of earlier times. Not in the remoteness of the mystery-temple was the beggar healed but on the highway of daily life. Not in the oblivion of sleep, without activity or consciousness of his own, was he made well but in the wakeful mood of everyday, contributing to the effort to help himself to that which was given him by Christ. Since that time the new Christian method of healing has neither become full-grown nor been rightly understood. All the elements which compose together the complete process of healing can be observed in the story of the blind man. In the future this process will become practical experience for many people, when sickness and healing will be understood in the Christian sense.

The blind man had become a changed person through and through. The neighbours, who had known him well, had to inquire if it was he. His answer was simply, "I am". These words are recorded in the Gospels of Christ, but at that moment they were spoken by a human being, by one whose name is not even known. The light of the world had kindled a spark of itself in this human soul. At this point, the authorities are introduced on the scene. The one-time beggar must answer their questions, which he does with calm and confidence. His parents refused to speak on his behalf, casting him off to fend for himself. The authorities rejected the healing. "We know that God spoke unto Moses, but this man, we know not from whence he is." The man who had been healed stood alone, but he gave a straight answer, putting them to shame with his courage. Where otherwise in the Gospels can someone be found who defended Jesus against the authorities but this nameless man, who had changed from a beggar into a hero, wise as the serpent, harmless as the dove? His encounters with the neighbours, the Pharisees and the parents made up the drama of a new birth in the human soul. With every question he was asked, the newborn self within him grew stronger and more capable. His mind wakened to active thinking, his heart to self-responsibility and devotion. At first he could say, "I am". Then he was able to stand face to face with the Pharisees through the power of the true self. Later he exerted in the cause of truth his will against theirs. They cast him out out and he stood there, rejected by parents and the community to which he belonged, lonely but upright in the strength of the Spirit within. Those who attacked him had in reality helped him to find himself, to pass through all the stages of the inner birth from self-awareness to self-responsibility and self-resolve.

He still did not know who had worked this change in him. First he spoke of the healer as "a man called Jesus", then as "a prophet". At last, in his loneliness, Christ came to meet him, bringing the comfort of enlightenment. He asked a question about the Son of God and gave the answer Himself. With that, the inner spiritual blindness of the nameless man was healed. He recognised the Son of God in Him who spoke. The quality of prophetic vision, which is faith, lighted up within him, and the responsible self, that had been born in his soul, received sight.

The threefold man was healed. When his bodily eyes were opened, that in him which came from the working of the Father-god was cured. When the true self was born in his soul and the light of his own thinking shone down into his willing, that was healed which partakes of the Son-god. When his spiritual insight was awakened, when he could say "Lord, I believe", the Spirit-god had entered his heart. Three times over he had been healed, in the name of Father, Son and Spirit.

When, in the ages of time before Christ's coming, people were cured of sickness, they were brought back into contact with the sphere of Paradise. Something of the old, unfallen nature of Man was infused into them again for their renewal. When Christ came, He performed another kind of healing. Through His own being, He brought to sick Humanity the ideal of Man made whole and consecrated to that which he should become. He called upon the vision, not of unfallen, but of resurrected Man. He summoned out of the future the forces of that which is not yet born into Mankind. The nameless blind beggar was born again, not to the innocence of childhood, but to the full-grown dignity of an upright, devoted man. Healing in the Christian sense is making whole, transforming the sick, disintegrated human nature into the wholeness which is true Man. It is the mystery of rebirth out of the state of being sick and weak with sin, into the new life that is born of the health-giving Spirit.

LENT

LENT

After Epiphany the next festival time in the Christian year is Lent. The period between the two has its particular meaning in the cycle of Christianity through the course of the year. It recalls the time of Christ's incarnation in Jesus, when He took on existence in the body and walked with men and women on earth. The many stories in the Gospels of the sayings and doings of Jesus Christ are the fitting content for thought and contemplation at this season. The picture of the God become Man fills our hearts and minds and awakens in us the vision of what earthly life can be when it is so transfigured. The evangelists record words which Christ spoke through a human mouth, journeys made on human feet, deeds done with human hands. Since then our bodies are dignified because He has once dwelt in flesh and blood, our ways on earth are hallowed because He has accepted them for Himself. In the season of the year when winter presses hard upon us, when conditions are apt to seem most burdensome, we are inspired by these pictures of earthly life transfigured by Him.

This experience is augmented and strengthened by a further one. Christ continues to take part in our existence here on earth, though in another sense than that described in the Gospels. His Spirit is continually with us, showing Himself to us in different ways. One of these consists in this, that we can become aware of a companion going with us along the path of life. When the trials and burdens seem too heavy, the strength too little, when a sense of helplessness invades us, the heart can feel, if it is sufficiently open, the nearness of Him who has made Himself acquainted with human burdens. Just when the weight of existence is naturally heaviest, this nearness is most readily to be felt. At all times and seasons the human heart can find the divine companion in earth-existence, but this season is naturally more favourable than others to the experience.

This period passes over into the season of Lent, which prepares the coming of Easter. By the time it begins the last of the winter is giving way to spring. The date of Lent varies with that of Easter. Unlike Christmas, which is fixed, the time of Easter follows the constellations in the sky, changing with the alternations of sun and moon. It is one of the last arrangements in our lives in which the movements of the heavenly bodies are reflected on earth. In earlier ages the influence of the stars in human lives was generally recognised, but now very few of the old customs are left except the movable festival of Easter. Even this has become a problem. Many people hold the view that a regular date fixed by law would be a practical convenience. The problem is in reality much greater. Should what is happening in the universe affect our existence on earth? Or is the world to be ruled only by business convenience? The date of Easter has become a touchstone by which we discover how far we are aware of being part of the whole universe and sharing its existence. The problem is nothing less than this.

According to the old custom of the Church, Lent should last for six weeks, during which life should proceed differently from the rest of the year. The sense of sin should be specially cultivated. More time should be given to spiritual exercises and fasting should be practised. For a long time now, Lent has acquired a disproportionate place in the Church year and has lost something of its true function, the preparation for Easter. The climax of the festival should be reached in the period that follows Easter Sunday, the forty days of resurrection lasting until Ascension. There is good ground nowadays for shortening the duration of

Lent to four weeks and for discovering new ways of giving this time the character of preparation. By such means its true relation to Easter would be restored.

Lent comes with the spring. It presents us with a great contrast between the kingdom of Nature and the inner state of the human soul. The plants and trees begin to grow and blossom. We human beings feel the increasing forces of life, but we cannot at once harmonise them with our own inner nature. How often is the first feeling of spring in our limbs a great weariness! How common it is for sick people to die with the opening of the crocus or the daffodils! The spring is in the first place the festival of the plants. The human soul does not find new life until the experience of death has been encountered and accepted on the way to the festival of resurrection. At this season the soul has to recognise a deep difference from Nature. The spring is not the beginning of new life within Man until Lent has changed to Easter.

Lent is the time for becoming aware of what is in truth always present in human life but half-hidden, destruction, death and evil. Destruction is continually with us. In the kingdoms of Nature the balance between growing and withering, between coming into being and destruction is held by the force of natural wisdom that holds sway throughout their existence. Of the seeds produced each summer, a proportion are prevented from germinating. Of the eggs laid, a number do not hatch. Of the young born to the animals, some perish before maturity. In the realms of human life, Nature can no longer hold the balance. Great powers of destruction have come under the direct control of human beings, who are not yet awake to the responsibility. On every hand, we see examples of chaos which people are producing through lack of wisdom. The condition of our contemporary world may seem dreadful to contemplate, but it is necessary to realise that the source of the trouble is in ourselves. Whether or not we are personally guilty, we should not avoid looking at that which affects the whole human community. By contemplating the disintegration around us, we shall find the longing stir within to discover the power to create anew out of the forces of human activity.

We encounter death from without and from within. We experience it from within as a force from which we never escape while we are alive on earth. At the end of our lifetime, when we shall stand at the threshold of a new life in another sphere, we shall face death from without. We shall recognise the dark force that has been secretly at work within us through all the years. We may be inclined to regard death as an enemy, but we owe much to its help in our present manner of existence. The balance in our constitution between the forces of life and death enables us to live and at the same time to think, to be active and at the same time to be aware of what we are doing. One side of our nature depends throughout life on the presence of death within. When life is over, we shall find ourselves overshadowed by the power of death, that comes from without. As the body falls completely into its grip, the eternal soul will pass out of its reach into the living sphere of the universe. It will find thereby release from the present state of existence and entry into the new. Death both within and without does us service but we come thereby with great dangers if its power is not kept in check, we are threatened with disintegration. In contemplating the mystery of its presence in our experience, we shall find a deeper understanding for the deed of Him who came to overcome death for our sake.

Evil as much as death accompanies us through our existence on earth. It may be easy to picture evil in the form of devils that come to tempt us, that make attacks from outside. When we do this, however, we are actually projecting outside something that is working from within. The tendency to wickedness is present in every human soul. The temptation to follow the bad nature within us is always there, the more so because our weakness will make it easy for us. Inner strength and effort are needed to make the Good real in our hearts and in our lives. The opportunity to create what is good is always at hand, but we are constantly beset by the temptation to give way to natural weakness. As an example, we have the experience of egotism. We are naturally egotists in the ordinary course of existence. It needs no effort, it comes of itself. But when we try to attain self-responsibility, to speak, to decide and act out of our true sense of self, then great inner activity and awareness are required.

It would not be possible for human souls to face the presence of death and evil within, constantly and clearly. From time to time, however, we should be able to put the veil aside, and Lent is the proper season. We come then to think of our human nature in some such way as this: I am aware of myself as a human being here in body on earth. But I am not what I am without the power of death existing in me and the force of evil working through my weakness. I cannot raise myself out of this state by my own strength. How do death and evil come to be so much part of me? As I am in my earthly being, I am empty and unfulfilled. Evil can enter that in me which is empty. I have become too much connected with death. I owe too much to this power, therefore I have become as I am. Only the presence of the Spirit within can fill me, will release me from the grip of death, will give me the strength to create the divine image within me. The spiritual man will be capable of redeeming the earthly man.

The mood of emptiness and longing for fulfilment in the Spirit is that of Lent. Awareness of death and evil is the source of the soul's longing. The true meaning of the overcoming of death at Easter is not comprehended unless this realisation has come about during Lent. The quality that is most necessary in observing this festival season is courage. That which is so much hidden at other times has to be faced. It is never easy to face facts, least of all the dark ones of the real existence of death and evil. It is easier to avoid them. Yet, the way through Lent to Easter is the way that Christ has gone through earth-existence. There is no other means of entering into this deed than to accept this inner experience, without drawing back, until we are led to the resurrection.

The World-Word became Man in Jesus Christ. He entered step by step into the destiny of Mankind on earth. He came into the presence of death and evil. They had no part in His being, for his nature was that of the Heavens, not as our ordinary human nature, part heavenly, part earthly. Though He was Himself free of them, He came to take on the life of Man and to enter out of freedom into their presence. His incarnation was a gradual descent into the depths, where they have power. The Temptation, which followed immediately on the baptism in Jordan, was the first moment of standing face to face with them. Thenceforth His earthly life was continually in their presence. The events of Holy Week were scenes from a drama that was reaching its climax. On the cross on Golgotha, during the descent into Hell, He suffered and wrestled with the spiritual powers of darkness. He grappled with and overcame that which threatened to consume and destroy human souls.

The Spirit of Christ dwells in the darkness that is spread over earth-existence by the beings who work death and evil. They continue to evolve their influence from age to age. In our time we experience how the darkness has penetrated human thoughts, until the mind's eye in many people is only capable of seeing matter in various forms existing by mechanical laws. Materialism is not merely a way of thinking or an attitude to life. It is a thick obscurity of spirit darkening human souls, blinding the inner eye, dulling the heart. It has a deadening effect, making existence flat and grey, robbing life of its meaning. It causes an eclipse in the spiritual life of modern times. But we need not be lost in tribulation, for the light of Christ is shining in the darkness. All those will find Him who learn in the shadows to seek the true light out of their own longing, who find in the emptiness the need for the meaning of existence.

In the course of the Christian festivals, Lent is the season in which our hearts dwell in the valley of the shadow of death. We face then what underlies our existence all through the year, the presence of evil and the infection of death within ourselves and in the world around. Once in the year, we stand in contemplation face to face with them, and we find in this experience that we are not alone in the valley of shadows. Christ is with us and He radiates the spiritual strength of light, life and love as the sun in the sky shines with external light.

THE PASSION

In the Gospel of St John the drama of Easter is introduced by a mysterious event, the raising of Lazarus from the dead. The brother of the two sisters, whose house in Bethany was visited at intervals by Jesus Christ, fell ill, died and was raised to life after his body had already been laid in the tomb. This event roused great public interest and prompted the Jewish priests to plan an attack on Jesus. Those readers of the Gospels, who have insight into the way in which they are written, recognise in the scenes from the story of Lazarus the pattern of the old ceremonial initiations which were performed in the ages of time before Christ's coming. These had been always held within the hidden precincts of the old temples. Lazarus was raised before the eyes of all the common people in a public place of burial. Whereas, in the old ceremonies, specially appointed high priests guided the candidates into the death-like sleep, lasting three days, and called them back to earth, Christ took the priestly office on Himself. He knew that the sickness of Lazarus was not an ordinary matter. He allowed it to take its course and guided from the distance the passing of the soul out of the body through the gate of death. Then He came and called back the soul to its earthly house.

Those present at this scene who understood what had happened were spiritually at a parting of the ways. Either they must recognise that the Messiah was in their midst, for no one besides He could openly perform the sacred act of death and life by strength within Himself. Or they must see a terrible blasphemy in what had been done, the work of a devil. An act of such spiritual importance performed before all the world was a challenge to a choice that could not be ignored. The cry had gone forth: who is not with Me is against Me.

Such was the outer aspect of the event. Inwardly it had another significance. The form of the old rites of initiation was followed so closely as to be unmistakable, although the stages of the ceremony were translated into acts of real life. Within the form, however, a different end was attained, because Christ Himself filled the office of the high priest. The old act of initiation had the effect of taking the soul out of the body into the spheres of the Divine World and bringing it back again in such a manner that memory-pictures were retained of what had been experienced. The soul of Lazarus passed away and out of his own strength could never have returned. In this sense Lazarus was in truth dead, for all candidates in temple initiations ran a real risk of dying. Christ called him back to earth to bring something with him different from the old kind of wisdom. His human soul was filled with what Christ brought in Himself to earth, to give to Mankind for the sake of the evolution to come. This was the indwelling power of the true self, the spiritual being enshrined in the human heart, set therein by Christ's own action. The first soul to be Christianised in this sense was that of Lazarus, who made himself so subject to the power and direction of his Master that he passed through death to new birth by His guidance. In such a manner he who had been Lazarus became the closest disciple, the firstborn of Christians, the one whom Jesus loved.

The inner significance of this event could only rouse the hostility of the Jewish priests as much as the outer, though they may well have been but dimly aware of it. The reign of their law, the régime in which human affairs were directed by authority from above, came in spiritual fact to an end. The new age began of the Spirit working from within. They were against what was beginning. They strove to kill what was new before it should have time to take root. They wished to hold Mankind back in the old ways of existence. In the drama of Easter we meet the great mystery that, among human beings whom Christ came to rescue and redeem, only a few recognised Him and others attacked Him. The Son of God was tortured and put to death by people for whose sake He descended into earth-existence.

Who were they who played the dark part in the world-drama of Easter? At the time of the festival of the Passover, Jerusalem was thronged with pilgrims coming to the Temple. A crowd of people were included in the scenes of Easter which opened with that of Jesus Christ's entry into the city riding upon the ass. In a flash of insight that passed through the whole multitude, they recognised that He had come for whom they and their forefathers had waited. They shouted: Hosanna, blessed is the King of Israel that cometh in the name of the Lord (St John, ch. 12). A little of the ancient faculty of second-sight, of seeing a degree further than the outer appearance, woke up in them. The humble ass became for them the token, spoken of by the prophets, by which they should know their king. Like the people represented in many of the old Greek dramas, they saw the God coming down into the dilemma of human affairs on earth. They poured out all the hope and enthusiasm of their hearts to Him. Jesus Christ had walked on earth for some time, but quietly, for the most part among small groups of people. On the road into Jerusalem He was shown to the multitudes. The Messiah appeared in such a manner that all could see and recognise Him.

Were these the same people who later cried to Pilate: crucify Him? The evangelist John speaks of priests and officers shouting these words, but the evangelist Mark says distinctly (St Mark, ch. 15) that the priests moved the people to ask for Barabbas to be released and Jesus crucified. In the picture drawn by John the people are silent, unwilling to protect Him whom they had hailed.

Not everyone in the crowd need be included, but it is scarcely possible not to imagine that the crowd who waved palm branches later betrayed Him. The flash of insight had passed. Having recognised Him with the help of old, expiring forces, when these later faded, the reaction set in strongly. One may imagine that disappointment made the crowd an easy prey to the priests. They had seen the God coming into their midst, but their world had not been changed and set right at a stroke. Then they saw Him who had come, a prisoner, accused by their own leaders and brought to judgement by the Roman governor. More than the old second-sight, which could only flare up for a moment, was needed to see in that abased figure the divinely-appointed Messiah. The multitude were too weak of soul to be capable of such insight. So it came about that they helped to put to death Him for whom they had waited with longing.

There were others also who shared in bringing about the passion and death of Christ. There were disciples, the one who betrayed and the other who denied Him. The circle of His twelve closest followers included one who sold his Master for thirty pieces of silver and gave Him into the hands of His enemies with a kiss. The evangelist John says that the devil put the betrayal into the heart of Judas (ch. 13). Satan, the prince of this world, was the great adversary of Christ in the Spirit. He needed a weak human will, through which to attack Him. Judas became his instrument. What within the heart of Judas made him open and willing to be used for this end? He had the same expectation of the coming of the Son of God as the others of his generation. He had the insight to distinguish Jesus Christ as the One who had the spiritual force and quality of the Messiah. In a different way, he had the same conviction as the Jewish priests.

The Messiah must act and behave as he, Judas, had every right to expect Him to do. He must save His people from oppression and establish His kingdom with might and glory in this world. Judas believed that what was done by the Messiah should conform to this world's standards. Did he not complain when the precious ointment was poured out in a symbolic rite? (St John, ch. 12.) His increasing dissatisfaction and impatience with his Master opened his heart's door to Satan. Did he at last resolve to call in force with the aid of the priests to put pressure on Him to reveal His power? Did disappointment and anger so blind him that he no longer realised what he was doing until, in the dark hour of the Crucifixion, he awoke again, to hang himself in despair? Whatever was his feeling, he lost himself so far that Satan could enter his will and make him the betrayer.

Peter was the first of the disciples who was inspired to say to his Master: Thou art the Son of God. But he became the one who denied him three times over on the night when He was taken prisoner by His enemies. Peter followed Him to the house of the high priest and was allowed to enter (St John, ch. 18). When he was asked by the girl who kept the door, by the soldiers and by a servant, if he were a disciple, he answered three times, no. Had he ventured so far and then become afraid? The drama of Easter, that was proceeding without pause or relief, was overwhelming for the disciples. They could not grasp what was happening. In one night they had sat with Him at supper, He had washed their feet and taught them the highest, clearest truth. They had been with Him in the garden and then seen Him betrayed, made prisoner and brought to trial. This all happened during the passover, the most dramatic festival of the Jewish year, at the close of an eventful week that had opened with the entry into Jerusalem. The disciples had not developed the strength of consciousness with which to understand and live in these events. The sense of himself, of who he really was and of that in which he believed, had faded and left Peter. His soul was dark and empty. He spoke truly when he said: I am not. When the cock crowed he remembered and came to himself. In bitter despair and shame, he crept away into hiding. He knew again who he was, but his inner strength was exhausted.

The priests and leaders of the Jews accused Him, tried Him, and clamoured for His death, forcing Pilate to pass the sentence. They were in authority over the people, whose whole history had been devoted to preparing for His advent. They rejected the Messiah, whom they intended to serve, overlooking the warnings of the Jewish prophets who had distinctly foretold in what guise He would appear. The manner of His coming and His way of behaviour were so entirely different from what they expected and wished that they turned against Him. How could it be, they must have felt, that He who called Himself the Son of God did not appear in their own ranks, making Himself their head, agreeing to their plans? Yet they were officers of the Temple, trained in its service, educated in the occult wisdom of the Hebrews. They were sensitive enough in spiritual matters to perceive that no ordinary prophet had appeared. They were not protected by the same obtuseness as the common run of people. Either they must recognise Him as the Messiah and abandon their assumptions and expectations, or they must destroy Him. So it came about that they, who should have known Him best, were His most bitter enemies.

The Roman governor, in whose power it lay to pass sentence of death, tried Jesus because He was delivered to him by the priests. Pilate had a shrewd insight into the character of Jesus and the behaviour of the Jews. He did not condemn Him to death out of bad will or stupidity. Yet he was tragically weak in the face of popular outcry and the threat to himself. In consequence he played one of the darkest parts in the drama of Easter against his own intention. The Roman soldiers, in their ignorance and brutality, shared his unhappy lot.

The trial of Jesus, especially as it is described by the evangelist John, shows the struggle of those who put Him to death. The Jewish priests were inspired by Caiaphas who, in his office of high priest, received a special illumination. It is said (St John, ch. 11) that he prophesied that one man should die for the people. He spoke to the other priests and the Pharisees with the voice of an oracle, revealing to them the will of God. Such prophesyings were always regarded as sacred, but they were open to much error of interpretation. The priests were, nevertheless, convinced that their purpose was divinely ordained. By contrast Pilate acted aimlessly and was continually in a state of doubt. He asked questions of his prisoner (St John, ch. 18): "Art thou a king?" and "What is truth?" The answers he received told him that which would have given him understanding for the drama in which he was unwillingly involved. "My kingdom is not of this world." He expected as ardently as the Jews that a God would become Man, but he could not listen to Christ's answers in all their earnestness. He heard, but he wanted further proof, a sign, or some show of authority that would convince everyone beyond doubt.

In his anxiety and uncertainty Pilate found himself publicly putting the Jewish priests to the test. Three times he gave them the opportunity to accept or reject Jesus Christ. Three times they rejected Him, and became each time more thoroughly and violently the enemies of the Messiah. First Pilate offered: "Will ye, therefore, that I release unto you the King of the Jews?" They answered: "Not this man, but Barabbas the robber." A second time Pilate brought Him forth in a kingly robe, crying: "Behold the man!" And they cried: "Crucify him!" They claimed the Law as their authority. The Law of Moses had been given by Jehovah to

His people. Now the people claimed it as their possession, to use as they would. They had chosen the robber and became themselves robbers of the Law's force, which rightly belonged to their god Jehovah. A third time Pilate said: "Behold your King", and they answered, "We have no king but Caesar!" They, who had been called by their God to prepare for the Messiah, rejected the Son of God who had become man and elected His opposite, the king of this world, who tried to make himself into a god. Then Pilate, unable, unwilling and afraid to choose between Christ and Caesar, delivered Him to be crucified.

The passion and death of Christ were brought about by human beings. The power of Evil had so far taken hold of men's souls that one disciple betrayed Him, the other denied Him, the leaders of the Chosen People intended to destroy Him and the Governor of the Romans, whose power then ruled the world, handed Him to His enemies. Those who so acted were not only playing their own part in the drama. They represented Mankind. They attacked Christ with all the dark forces of greed, fear and hatred of the Spirit with which human souls have been infected by the poison of Evil. He, who came to rescue and redeem men, was hated, rejected, and killed by them. Nor did He resist. He accepted hate, pain and death at human hands. He did not refuse the Passion, but He laid hold of it and transformed the suffering into the means of bringing about that which no human imagination could foresee. The divine power, to which He had earlier refrained from giving an earthly expression, was then poured out in the effort to master suffering and win from it the strength to bring life out of death.

Christ accepted the Passion and transformed it into the victory over matter. He forgave those who treated Him with hatred, neither blaming nor wishing to punish them. In a much greater sense He forgave the whole of sinful Mankind, wresting salvation for human beings out of their deed of rejection. Since that time, the destiny that human beings made for Him has become their own. We must tread the way of salvation if we would partake in the Resurrection of Man. The way goes through the Passion, through suffering and the experience of death. We cannot become that which we shall be if we shrink from treading this way. In the darkness there shines the light. In the shadow of death, the compassionate figure is seen of Him who is our divine companion on the way, which He Himself has trod.

THE CROSS

The greatest of Christ's deeds, that on which Christianity is founded, was performed on the cross, in the place of the skull, Golgotha. The crucifixion is described truly as a deed, but, looked at from outside, the scenes pictured by the four evangelists would seem to show human beings in action and Jesus Christ as the sufferer accepting what they did without resistance. So, from one side, it was. Yet the Gospels allow the mind's eye to penetrate to the other side and to behold how the suffering of the cross was transformed by Christ into the deed of Spirit for which the whole universe was waiting. He accepted the judgement of men, of the priests, of Pilate, of the crowd in the streets, and He suffered the agony caused by human hands, by the soldiers who tortured His body and nailed it to the cross. He was not reduced by pain to the level of the victim, who loses himself in what he has to bear. At the trial He had said to Pilate: "thou wouldst have no power against Me, except it were given thee from above" (St John, ch. 19, v. 11). He accepted the suffering as inevitable to that which He had come to achieve and He changed it to His own purpose. The force of the pain, which was intended to destroy Him by those who inflicted it, became an element in the creative deed of the cross.

Many representations have been made of the pain of Christ's passion and crucifixion, in painting, carving and in words The stations of the cross have been for centuries an object of meditation and intense experience of feeling by those who considered it important to enter imaginatively into this event. In our time a new level of consciousness should be reached, which can only come through increased understanding of the Passion. This is not an attempt to minimise the suffering. On the contrary, it appears greater and deeper than the human heart can well comprehend. Nevertheless, it should be understood in relation to the whole deed of Golgotha and then the danger is avoided that the heart is overwhelmed by the contemplation of pain.

When Christ became Man, He took upon Himself an existence of suffering. The material world had not been His abode before, nor had He known the burden and limitation of the body. His divine being could only experience human existence on earth as suffering. The process of His incarnation, which began at the baptism in Jordan, lasted until the cross. The divine and human parts within Him, the God and the man, penetrated each other gradually. So opposite had human nature become to the divine, that it was a kind of crucifixion from within. The pain of the cross was the culmination of what had gone before. In the experience of the crucifixion Christ penetrated to the ultimate depths of human nature and became one with Man. It was suffering beyond what human imagination can grasp. In that hour the incarnation was fulfilled and became the central fact of human history.

When in Holy Week we remember His passion and death, we find the courage to contemplate the suffering, in part at least, if we begin to understand its creative meaning. We cannot ignore the tragedy that human hands and hearts inflicted the pain, the destiny of which Mankind must bear ever since, but we should look beyond. Christ overcame pain, making therefrom the instrument for the deed which He had come to earth to perform. Another picture of the crucifixion should now take the place of those so well known in past centuries, which show the tortured body, the helpless head, the limbs coloured with decay. The cross is a true fact of history, which should in no way be concealed, but the figure of Him who hangs thereon should be one in whom suffering is accepted and transformed, in whom the Spirit creates new life out of pain. Christ overcame the cross in the very act of crucifixion. The light of His Spirit shone in the darkness of suffering and death. He transformed what was done to His hurt into the substance of His divine deed.

The crucifixion was the point of the deepest incarnation of the Christ-being into manhood. At that moment He descended into death. What, then, is death? It is the state of separation from the Divine World. Where is death to be found? Though this is more than half hidden from us in our lifetime, the earth is the place where separation from God truly exists. In the heights of the Heavens from which Christ came, death is an unknown mystery which could be sought only in the far country of the earth. Mankind lives in the midst thereof without realisation until the hour in which the soul stands at the gate of death that leads into divine life. Christ, being God, entered into the depths of human nature on the cross and passed down into the realm of death, into the place of existence empty of the Divine. He invaded the void of separation, to overcome it.

Christ's entry into death was different from all human dying. It was undergone in the fullness of His divine consciousness. It was an act from which creation could begin anew. It was death, in which divine birth took place. As Jesus Christ died in human form on the cross, the creating God was born into the realm of the earth. He came to make the place where death is real into His kingdom of Life. He chose to be born as God into this world through the death on the cross. The scene on Golgotha is a double mystery, death in birth and birth in death. The mystery which we celebrate on Good Friday contains both the darkness of death and the light of the spirit-birth in the picture of the cross.

The four Gospels record seven sayings of Jesus Christ during the crucifixion. They do not explain what was happening, but they are like seven windows through which we can get glimpses into the universal mystery which was enacted. The two aspects of death and birth are to be found interwoven in each of these sayings, and to look at them from this point of view gives illustration to this conception of the cross.

The first is recorded by St Luke: "Father, forgive them, for they know not what they do" (St Luke, ch. 23, v. 34). So Christ speaks of the soldiers whose hands nailed His body to the cross. Spoken at this moment on Golgotha, this saying can be understood in the widest sense. It is said of the Roman soldiers, but not only of them. It may be taken to include those standing round, those who had already tried and condemned Him, and also those who from the crowd in the streets had cried: crucify Him. All who were against Him, who failed to recognise Him, whether then or throughout the centuries that have followed, are included. From a still wider angle, it would be true to hear these words said of all human souls, even those who seek to follow Him, for in each one lives the power to betray what one loves. The crucifixion is the betrayal of the Son of God by all Mankind, whom He had come to help. The soldiers were not acting for themselves but for Mankind as a whole, out of the hatred and opposition to the world of God which is the fruit of the fall of Man. Christ accepted human hate. He allowed Himself to be put to death by Man for Man's sake.

In the scene of the crucifixion we see in the crowd of people gathered round those who are present on behalf of Mankind. The picture is not complete unless the background is as full of witnesses as the foreground. The whole of the heavenly hosts should be pictured there, angels, archangels and the company of all the spiritual beings who are members of the being of God. They look downwards from their kingdoms in the Heavens to behold the mystery of the Son of Man hanging on the cross, descending into the shadows of death. In this first saying Christ turns to speak to the all-being of the Father. He prays on behalf of Mankind. The lost child of the universe is Man, who has fallen so deeply into sin and death as to reject the divine messenger from the Heavens. Christ prays that men and women shall be forgiven because of their ignorance and weakness. These words may be understood as a request that Man shall not be left to fall further and further away from God until he is swallowed up in separation and death. The Son brings with these words the lost children back to the Father and prays that they may be received into the community of the Heavens. The answer to the prayer is contained in its making. The new half of Man's history begins, when Christ on the cross leads the human souls into the presence of the Father and prays for them.

The second saying is likewise recorded by St Luke (ch. 23, v. 43). Two malefactors hang on each side of His cross. One is angry and expects that Christ will use miraculous powers to save Himself and them. The other is changed in his heart by the presence of the One in the centre, recognising His innocence and their guilt. He asks to be remembered in His kingdom and hears the answer: "today shalt thou be with Me in paradise". Christ entered through the cross into the sphere of death, and at the same time into the region of sin. Not by His own guilt, but in innocence through strength of Spirit, He went into the place where sinfulness is experienced and has its consequences. The one sinner asks to be released from sin and pain. The other recognises that Man has come into the grip of evil through his weakness and guilt. He prays that he may pass through the dark region of evil, into which he has come, and find the way into the kingdom of light.

The two malefactors speak to the One who shares their condemnation and He answers the prayer. He promises to open the gate to Paradise. In that moment Man is no longer condemned to be still further imprisoned in evil, to become increasingly helpless in sin. The promise is not that the souls of men and women shall be miraculously released from temptation and evil, but that the gate of Paradise shall be opened, that a new stream of goodness may flow through them. Sinfulness is something to be overcome, a sickness that gives pain until it is healed. Christ accepted on the cross the sinfulness of Man and the presence of evil. He brought the power of healing into the place of sin and gave with His words to the repentant malefactor the promise of living medicine to make whole the inner being of Man.

The third saying comes from the Gospel of St John (ch. 19, v. 26). Only one of the disciples, John, was able to bear the sight of the cross, but some of the women were there, in the company of the mother of Jesus. Those who could not find the strength to be present felt the fear of condemnation, suffering and death. Those who were able to stand at the foot of the cross could pass beyond fear and take part in the event of birth which happened in the midst of death. They could behold the light of His Spirit shining in the darkness, and a beam of its creating force touched them. Jesus Christ said to the Mother, indicating the disciple whom He loved standing by: "Woman, behold thy son." To the disciple He said: "Behold thy mother." He created with these words a new relationship between them. Later, at the first Whitsuntide, the Mother was with the twelve apostles when the Holy Spirit descended upon them. The saying from the cross does not merely represent an act of human kindness. It is the birth from the Spirit of a new relationship of the heart between men and women.

In the first age of Man's history, up to the coming of Christ, the tie of blood had been the source of most human relations. Love and hate had followed the promptings of the blood, of tribal and racial sympathy and antipathy. The history of Mankind had then been a progressive coming down to the earth and the blood relationships had been a means of helping the souls on their way down. At the cross a new force of spiritual love entered the hearts of the disciple and the mother. They were not brought together by the urge of the blood but by the creative word of Christ. They found each other as mother and son by reason of the wellspring of love which began in that hour to flow within their being. Such relationships of the spirit help human souls in the progress of the second, Christian half of Man's history, which is the way from the earth back to the Divine World.

The fourth word from the cross (St John, ch. 19, v. 28) is: "I thirst". The descent of Christ into the physical body, into the region where want and temptation are felt, is accomplished in this saying. The intensity of human need and longing is expressed. The vinegar on the sponge, that is offered by human hands, is accepted. When thirst, which is the token of Man's separation from God, in whom his existence began, is felt by Christ, it is transformed. Hunger and thirst come from the fallen nature of Man, are part of the original curse brought upon him by the temptation of the devil. Yet thirst for the Divine is a constant reminder to the human soul of that from which it is separated. Longing is the force that saves a human being from resignation, from living only as a creature of earthly circumstances. Thirst is transmuted by Christ into the power of salvation, into that which wakens the human heart and drives it on to seek the way onwards to the kingdom of the Spirit. The heart that feels no thirst is deadened. The thirsting heart finds the helping company of Him who passed through the pain of death on the cross, on the way of transformation that leads into the presence of God.

The fifth saying is that which is recorded as the only one by St Matthew (ch. 27, v. 46) and St Mark (ch. 15, v. 34): "My God, My God, why hast Thou forsaken Me?" These words were not spoken for the first time. They were taken from the beginning of Psalm 22, which describes the crucifixion in prophecy. They are human words on the lips of Christ, spoken from the depths into which He had penetrated, from the dark place of separation from God. In speaking them, He takes on Himself the destiny of Man as His own burden. He carried the creating power of His Spirit into human existence on earth. The state of separation from the Divine, which is sin and death, is transformed. It is not ended, wiped out or prevented. It undergoes change, becoming not a curse but an opportunity. One reality unknown to the beings of God, who have their existence in the community of the Divine World is freedom. Without separation from the Heavens, there is no freedom. The human soul, who knows god-forsakenness, can develop the capacity of becoming free. Man, the creature of God, can become the friend and fellow-worker in freedom with the Divine World.

The sixth saying in the traditional order is from St John (ch. 19, v. 30): "It is finished." Another interpretation of the word would be: it is accomplished. Christ came from the heights of Heaven down into the world of earth to seek Man, the lost child of God in the place of separation. He came as the messenger of the Divine World to discover the mystery of death and confront the powers of evil. The path of His experience went through incarnation into a human body and the suffering of the cross. Step by step He had passed along the way He had chosen. Then came the hour for the body to be laid aside, for the Spirit to leave the cross. The will of God had been performed by His Son. "It is fulfilled." Yet this is not the end of Christ's work. One stage is completed. What is to follow will be the descent into Hell and the resurrection. While the incarnation is ending, the new mystery is beginning, through which the Spirit of Christ takes the earth into Himself and bears onwards its life into the future. The descent of the Son of God is transformed into the ascent of Man and of the earth. Out of the accomplishment of the one, the other is evolved. The passing into death is completed, that life may rise anew.

The last saying is from St Luke (ch. 23, v. 46): "Father, into Thy hands I commend My Spirit." This word, like the first, spoken to the Father in the Heavens, describes the passing of Christ out of the body into death. Dying means for human souls going from the earth into the heavenly realms of the Father-god. In the truest sense it means being given into His hands. When Christ died on the cross, He did not return to the Divine World. He passed into the kingdom of death below the sphere of the earth's surface which is the field of our human life, where we only feel indirectly the influences of death. He went into the depths beyond our existence, taking the opposite direction to that towards the Heavens. He descended by His own strength of Spirit into the void, bearing the divine presence into the place where God was not. There He withstood the powers that wield the force of death. In the last stage of His deed on Golgotha He strove to face death and overcome it. When we contemplate what is expressed in the last saying, our inner eye should again look into the heights and see the image of the Father, in whom are comprehended all the company of Heaven. Then we behold how the arms of the Father reach into the depths, embracing the whole universe and how Christ is born in His hands into the kingdom of death itself, that there may be quickened the new life.

THE DESCENT INTO DEATH

After the death upon the cross, the body of Jesus was laid into the tomb of rock in the garden near to the hill of Golgotha. Later, when the women came early on Easter morning to anoint it, the stone at the tomb's entrance was rolled away and the body had disappeared. What had happened?

The material body of Jesus had been the dwelling place for the Spirit of Christ. After three years had passed, He no longer required such a mode of existence and His Spirit left the bodily sheath in the hour when He died on the cross. That which He had laid aside was ready to be given over to one for whom it was a much needed gift. The earth, the living being of the planet which we inhabit, was waiting to take the sacred body to herself. The corpses left by all human souls pass over into the being of the earth, by whatever means they go into dissolution. In a sense they are her food, refreshing her withering existence. Their quickening virtue comes from the formative forces that are released as their substance decays. Such forces have streamed down from the universe and maintained the bodies while they were alive. They have come from beyond the earth, therefore they can nourish her, when her own strength weakens. Such a process is happening continually, but when the body of Jesus was put into the tomb a much greater and more dramatic change was effected in the life of the earth.

The indwelling Spirit of Christ had gradually transformed the substance of flesh and blood through the years of the incarnation. Even the nature of the bones had been altered. As human beings, we go through life divided between the differing natures of soul and body. We never completely master their limitations. The Spirit was so powerful within the being of Christ that the fleshly house was transformed, even in its bony skeleton, where the hardening forces of death are strongest. Cosmic strength, giving new life to her existence for times to come, was received by the earth with this spiritualised body. After it had been laid into the rocky tomb and embalmed with spices that assisted the process of dissolution, the ground was shaken by an earthquake. One may imagine the tomb as the earth's mouth opening in the earthquake to receive the communion of His body. The shroud remained as a sign that no thief had removed it. The dissolving substance of flesh and bone, which had been impregnated with the forces of Christ's being, were the consecrated host given to the earth for her communion.

Before the entombment, while the body still hung on the cross, the blood flowed from Christ's wounds and from His side down into the ground. As the body became the bread in the earth's communion, so the blood was the wine. The cosmic forces of Christ came from the spiritual being of the sun. The earth had lost much of the strength of life which she had from the creation at the beginning. Extinction threatened her. She was liable to become a corpse in the universe. Then Christ offered Himself as a sacrifice for her existence. The blood flowed from the cross, bearing the spiritual power of the sun into her being. Her evolution was enabled to continue until now and into the future. A hidden treasure of golden life had been stored within her. We are still unaware of what it will bring forth in the future but it is the source of the earth's hope of resurrection. She should, through the Saviour who gave her the store of lifegiving virtue, become another sun. She who was already far on the way to the state of a world-corpse, has been given the secret power to become, like the sun, a giver of life to the universe.

When, at Eastertide, we watch the unfolding of the spring, the budding, the shooting, the bringing forth, we see new life springing out of decay. We are seeing the shadow of death and resurrection. Behind lies the reality, the living fact of Christ's death and His rising to life. Without it, the spring would long ago have ceased, for the earth would have been extinct. The spring is not the symbol of resurrection, it is the abiding reminder that the earth's life, which dies down in the winter, is renewed again from the spiritual wellspring which her Saviour has opened within her by His own deed.

When Christ died upon the cross and his body was given to the earth, He entered in spirit upon the struggle with the powers of death. It is easy to imagine that, since He was the Son of God come down from the Heavens, He would as a foregone conclusion achieve that which he intended. In fact, this was not so. The evolution of the world is full, to use very human language, of the risks taken by God. The ultimate future of Mankind is still uncertain. Human souls are still left to make their choice between the way of Christ and that of the prince of this world. Unthinking and unknowing as most people are, a large part of world-destiny is in their hands. When one contemplates this fact, one has a flash of insight into that which the Divine World has risked by offering the Son for the salvation of Mankind. Such a conception is necessary to realising what took place at the descent of Christ into the realm called Hell.

The region where the real power of death lies is under the surface of our earthly life. Its influence penetrates our existence. We are aware of it, we rely upon it, but we rarely have to face its naked reality. We divine it in the hardness of the ground under our feet, in the firmness of our own skeleton. We feel its touch in the crumbling of the rocks, the withering of flowers, in the extinction of animals. We know its grip on ourselves, the hardening of the body in age and the weariness of spent forces. Ahead of us looms the threat of that moment when its cold grip will be stronger than the body's vitality and the spirit will be obliged to change house. Nevertheless, death is constantly covered up by life, and we do not see it face to face. We keep to the surface of things and avoid the occult reality beneath us, the real presence of death that has come about through the separation from the Divine World of God. Emptiness of the Divine has become a positive force, wielded by dark beings of a spiritual nature.

We human beings walk in the valley of the shadow of death throughout our earthly existence. The Sons of God, who inhabit the spheres of the Heavens, have never known death. It was for them a dark mystery, which they could not solve. All the wisdom they could give to human souls in their destiny on earth never included this riddle, for which there was no answer in the Heavens. When the Son of God became man, He came as the first of the gods into the region where death is to be encountered. He took upon Himself the task of passing below the surface of earth-existence, where death and life mingle, and of entering the dark void where emptiness of the Divine had become the cold reality of death. He confronted the prince of this world and struggled with him. He strove with His divine strength to overcome the force of emptiness, to carry the divine light into this darkness and let it shine again out of the depths. And He prevailed. Since this descent and the time of His struggle, the power of death is no more independent of the godhead. Death is not destroyed: it is overcome and restrained. It has been made a force to be used in the universe. It has been robbed of the sting of almightiness and taken from the independent power of the adversary.

At the time when the Spirit of Christ passed into the region of death, the souls of men and women who had died had come into a tragic state. In the early ages of Mankind's history, when human souls were still so near to the Divine World that they could throughout their lifetime recollect their existence therein before birth, they had returned to their homeland of the Spirit at death. As the world of earth became in time much more separated from the Heavens and the souls forgot their place of origin, the return became more difficult. Instead of entering the community of the spiritual beings and dwelling in the many mansions of the starry spheres, they were imprisoned in the region where the pictures of the past life on earth surround those who have died. They found themselves in a land of shades, where they were aware of being only the shadows of their former selves. Hades, or Hell, was the old name for the realm of shadows where the souls met the tragic experience of death.

When Christ died, He came to the imprisoned souls of the dead and, having overthrown the prince of death, He wrought a transformation in their existence. He released them from the land of shades and gave them the strength to go on into the worlds of the Father. There they could find the experience of the universe, out of which their being had been born at the beginning of creation, and the healing of the infirmities caused by the sickness of sin. Since then, Christ has become the guide of human souls on the journey between this and the other world. He takes them into His care and goes with them to the dark Gate of Death, showing them the light shining from the other side, leading them out into the eternal realms of the Father. Each one will take the path of experience through the region where he sees the pictures of his past life. When this is completed, he will be prepared to ascend to the heights of the universe and find his home in the many mansions of the stars. There he will be healed and refreshed by the divine wisdom that will shine upon him in the manifold forms in which it lives in the starry constellations.

By His descent into Hell, Christ changed the destiny of the souls of the dead. He won from death also another gift for Mankind. In the course of time since the interference with Man's life on earth by the powers of evil began, the souls of human beings had become wrongly related to their bodies. At the beginning, when the whole community of the sons of God were occupied in creating Man, they brought forth the spiritual idea on the pattern of which all human bodies are built. As every building is constructed on a plan conceived in the mind, so each body, in spite of personal variations of every kind, is formed on the idea that originated in the creative mind of God. This primaeval divine idea is expressed by the poet Blake as "the human form divine". The substances of the body, those which compose bones, muscles, flesh, and all the material parts, are ordered and formed by this pattern, which is common to all human beings, although varied by each one according to his character. It is the abiding part, continually gathering and releasing the material substances in the process of decay and renewal, which never ceases while the soul lives in the earthly house. The spiritual entity of the body gives to the soul the experience and capacities that it derives from bodily existence. The material content may be more obvious to us, but in fact the spiritual human form is that upon which we depend throughout our earthly life.

The beings of Evil were able, after the fall of Man into their power, to distort the relation between body and soul. The human body ceased to be wholly that which was intended and foreordained among the sons of God. In consequence, its pattern was affected. No longer was it capable of taking in and losing again material substance without effect on itself. The process of building up the substantial content of the body is carried out by the forces of salt, that have the virtue of crystallisation. They are capable of fixing substance and building it in shape. Other forces in the body have the capacity to destroy substance and to turn it into ash, from which the power of life has been burnt out entirely. Before Christ came to earth, human bodies had sickened in such a manner that the divine pattern had a tendency to become attached to the ash-producing forces. The salt-forces were capable of producing processes of solution and dissolution so that the "human form divine" is untouched. Those which produce ash, on the other hand, had the effect of pulling the spiritual part down into matter, where the grip of death could seize upon it. The divine idea of Man in bodily form was no longer free from the forces of decay. It became, as time went on, increasingly entangled with the processes of destruction to which material substances are subject.

When the Spirit of Christ descended into the realm where the presence of death is real and true, He had the strength to hold together and save from disintegration the "human form divine", which had, as He died on the cross, separated from the earthly frame of flesh and bone. Christ rescued and renewed the bodily pattern of Man, doing so not for Himself alone but for all human souls. The risen body, in which He appeared later to the apostles when He ate with them (St Luke), was the ideal human form, unaltered and undisguised by personal variation. It was real in the physical sphere but had become independent of material substance. Capable of changing substances in the process of digestion (St Luke), it was nevertheless free from material limitations, passing, for instance, through closed doors (St John). It was not the body of Jesus as it had been before the crucifixion and was therefore not easily to be recognised. It was the "human form divine" walking on earth. Each one who met Him who had risen from death beheld the pattern of his own future body, which the soul that follows Christ will wear at the end of the world.

Crucifixion, descent into the presence of death and of the powers of Evil, and Resurrection are the deeds of Christ, through which He has transformed the life of Mankind and of the world.

His creating power does not fail and His Spirit is here with us in our midst. Looking into the future in the light of Easter, we see the path of human destiny stretching ahead. It is the way which He knows, because He has made it His own. Through the valley of the shadow of death it leads, between the temptations of the Evil Ones, into the bright light of the Resurrection of Man that lies, if we follow with faithfulness, at the end of the world.

EASTER

EASTER

The climax of Lent is Holy Week, the days during which Christ's passion is repeated in our contemplation, until on Good Friday the hour of His death is reached. Holy Saturday is the time of His descent into Hell, the realm over which the power of death rules. In the night which leads over from Saturday to Sunday comes the great turning point of the drama and the dawn of Easter morning brings the beginning of the Resurrection. The festival time of Easter lasts until Ascension Day, which follows forty days later. Nowadays it is often the custom to observe only the holiday period of the first Sunday and Monday. In reality Easter should be celebrated through all the days of resurrection in remembrance of the time when the Risen One walked and talked with the disciples.

Each year at Eastertime one can have again the experience that the festival is not an entirely human matter, that the sun, the earth, the plants and the animals, are remembering and observing it. The weather usually expresses something of the mood, but the feeling of the Easter days comes from a deeper, less changeable sphere. Out in the countryside on Good Friday there is a widespread hush, the solemn stillness of contemplation. The mood can be felt in all weathers, as if the oncoming spring would pause and be hushed in remembrance of the cross. The original day of the crucifixion was dark and tragic. The sun's light was eclipsed, earthquake shook the ground and horror spread through the realms of Nature. Today the quiet of remembered tragedy has taken the place of disturbance. The sense of Nature holding her breath and waiting in solemnity can usually be felt throughout Holy Saturday. On Easter Day there is a rush of joy and new life. The spring goes forward, sometimes at a bound. The sun's strength waxes, the buds hasten to open into leaf and flower, the songs of the birds are triumphant. The earth so clearly observes Easter that it is hard to imagine how people can suppose that they might fix the date according to their own wishes.

It is good to watch Nature keeping the festival, for, in truth, without the first Easter, the spring would long ago have ceased to come back to the earth. We usually assume that Easter is a festival held in the spring. Actually, since the coming of Christ, the original event of Easter is the origin of the spring that returns each year. The earth was far on the way to decay and destruction, when He came and brought a fresh stream of cosmic life to renew her existence for the second half of evolution. In the mystery of Easter, He united His spiritual Being with the earth's life and soul for all time to come. Living joy flows through the airy expanses above, renewed strength is poured out from the sun at Eastertide. The earth is born again in the spiritual presence of Christ and feels the gladness of her quickened life.

The renewal of Man's being is celebrated at Easter with that of the earth. New strength streams into the pulse of his life. His blood flows with fresh force, his breath is inspired with comfort. No longer is the contrast felt between the oncoming spring without and the emptiness of Man's inner nature. The risen Christ brings new spiritual life into the heart of Man and into the streaming of breath and blood. Man's earthly nature is an organ for the Spirit. Its existence is empty and dark without the spiritual reality of the self within. The sense of self becomes egotistical, the soul withers, the inner nature is filled with darkness, until Christ pours into Man's being the spiritual essence of the true self. Then the blood streams in fulfilment, the breath draws in life from the universe for the comfort and strength of the soul. That which then flows when he speaks from within Man into the world outside is quickened by the Spirit's power. In the time of passion and death before Easter, the soul of Man, cut off from the spheres of the Spirit, and menaced by the powers of evil, experienced sorrow and spiritual want.

At the festival of the Resurrection, the soul of Man becomes aware that the empty place within is hallowed by the presence of his true Spirit. The inner void is filled with the creating fire, which shall be the lasting source of spiritual activity within him. The Risen One has chosen the soul to be the sanctuary wherein He lays His divine power. He would raise Man, by this working within from death of soul to life in the Spirit. He would prepare him to return to the worlds of the Father as a being resurrected in the pattern of His resurrection. What He achieved in Himself at Easter, He would perform within Man in the ages of evolution to come. In His work of resurrection, He offers to the universe that which has not yet been part of its existence. In the sick and sinful being of Man, He creates what the Heavens will receive in the fullness of time as the new offering made from the earth, where out of death life is won and out of sickness healing. He who offered Himself to Man will offer redeemed Man to the divine world of God.

Easter is the festival of our fulfilment as children of Mankind, of the rescue of our earthly existence from aimlessness, and the renewal of its purpose and meaning. All the other festivals of the year take their significance from the Mystery of Golgotha. The whole of Christianity has its meaning in the fact of the Resurrection. Nevertheless, the experience of Easter is not given to us human beings in the natural course of events as the spring is given to Nature. The deed of Christ has been done and is continued in our own time. We live even in our physical existence largely by grace of what He has performed.

Yet we know little of Easter unless we awaken to its mystery in our hearts. As Golgotha was the greatest event of all time, so it is the one that makes the greatest demand upon our understanding. It requires to be celebrated with all our powers of thinking. We may follow in deep feeling the transition from Good Friday to Easter Sunday and keep the holy mood of the days of resurrection, but we shall not feel that we have really caught more than the shadow of Easter in this way. Each year our thinking should penetrate a little further into this most profound of mysteries, the understanding of which will last us more than this lifetime. No festival requires so much power of thought in its celebration as Easter.

One method of deepening the understanding of the event of Golgotha is to follow in contemplation what happened between the entry into Jerusalem on Palm Sunday and the Resurrection on Easter morning, as if one were watching the scenes of a great mystery play. So indeed it was. Christ enacted on earth at the first Easter the greatest drama of human history. Before His coming, in the mystery temples, rituals had been performed in which certain chosen men passed in a drama of the soul through death and new birth into the world of the Spirit. Outside the temples a selection of these rituals was shown to the mass of the ordinary, uninitiated people in sacred plays that were performed in accordance with the seasons of the year. When Christ came, He fulfilled what had been done in prophecy through ritual and drama, and performed the deed of death and life as an historical event on the stage of the earth. That which had been foreshadowed in human souls became a fact, both physical and spiritual, in the history of the world. What was done by Christ was in every detail a true expression in earthly existence of spiritual realities. So it comes about that a real experience of Easter may be found by pondering in the thinking heart the scenes of the mystery-drama which are described in the Gospels. Each day of Holy Week has its appropriate scene. One may feel oneself to be watching a play that takes many days to perform. All that one has been able to learn of Christianity in the whole year is needed to help one to comprehend and find the meaning of what is seen by the mind's eye. The stories in the four Gospels are not all alike, particularly those that describe what happened on the day of resurrection. It is not necessary to try to fit them all together into one coherent picture. There is much more value in contemplating one after the other and allowing oneself to look through the eyes of each evangelist in turn at the mystery which is beyond the confines of any single description. Just the differences illuminate the event from many sides.

Such a contemplation of the Easter drama opens the heart to see that the event is not only the centre of history for Mankind and for the earth. From the other side, from that of the Heavens and the beings who dwell therein, it is likewise the decisive deed performed at the turning point of time. Thinking of Easter, the human soul finds himself in community with angels, archangels and all the company of Heaven. He sees the veil between the two worlds open and finds that the hierarchies of the heavenly world are his companions. Christ's coming to earth, His deed on Golgotha have been described as an act of divine freedom. It was resolved upon by the whole community of divine beings who dwell in the kingdom of God. The Father-god bears within Himself many spiritual beings who are members of Him and who do His will in the universe. They all looked from the spheres of Heaven down to the fallen world of earth and beheld Man, the prodigal son of God. The compassion of the Divine Father moved them to the will to help and to save. The chief among them offered Himself and by a common decision was sent from the house of the sun into the far dark country of the earth. From the distance they followed Him upon His course. They looked towards Golgotha, watching His entry into the mystery of death, which was unknown to them in their own spheres. They are present in the drama of Easter, looking down from the heights. Behind them are stretched out the arms of the Father Himself, enfolding within them the round world, reaching even into the depths. The cross stands within the circle of the Father's being and the will flows from Him into the act of redemption. The earth is the place where the deed of Christ is done. The prodigal children of humanity are those for whom it is performed. The will of the divine World of the Father is the power and might with which the Son overcomes death with life.

The Resurrection is the second birth of Christ into the existence of the earth. At His incarnation He descended from the heights of the Heavens into the body of a man. At His resurrection He ascended from the depths of death in the spirit-body, which is the "human form divine" redeemed from destruction. Since that time His Spirit dwells with the earth, His influence weaves and works in the evolution of Mankind. The Resurrection is the source of the continuing stream of creative power which flows from His presence into the life of our world. In each age, in our own time, He is spiritually present and at work. In the weaving of history there are signs that He is here. In the flame of the Spirit that burns in the depths of the human heart, He is here. In the renewed life of the earth that breathes through the rhythm of the seasons, He is here. Today there are times when one or another person, perhaps someone whose thoughts often turn to Him, perhaps someone who has never used the name, looks up to find that a stranger is beside him. The stranger is beside him. The stranger is not quite unknown. Though He is unexpected, He touches hidden memories which the heart has known before it could remember. He awakens hope that the heart has almost abandoned for shame at its own inadequacy. He kindles faith and vision, through the enthusiasm for ideals that shine beyond us in times still to come. Then the one who has seen knows: He is here.

The deed of Golgotha was not ended with Christ's rising from the dead. What was then begun continues until today. The powers that set up the cross which He accepted are still at liberty to spread their influences. In a modern form, in the materialism of today in the most comprehensive sense, He encounters the death-bringing forces that threaten Mankind's spiritual destruction. The experience of the cross is not yet ended in the world. But the power of the Resurrection does not fail. In the chaos of the present time human souls can find the life that has overcome death, can behold more clearly than before the light that shines in the darkness. Easter is a mystery continuing through the ages of time. It is the clue to the meaning of our life on earth and the promise of what should be fulfilled in times to come.

THE RESURRECTION

In the night of Easter, Christ rose again. Those who came in the early dawn of the morning on the first day of the week found the empty tomb and heard the news of His rising. The four separate stories of the Resurrection told in the four Gospels are accounts of what different people experienced on Easter day. None of the evangelists have attempted to set down a comprehensive statement of what actually happened. Each one has reported certain scenes relating to the event. St Matthew describes what two women and some soldiers saw and heard at the tomb and what the eleven disciples experienced at a later time on a mountain. St Mark tells of three women going to the sepulchre and of what befell them. The following passage in this chapter is a summary of what is told by the other evangelists. St Luke's story is longer. First he describes a crowd of women at the tomb, followed by Peter, then the two disciples on their walk to the village of Emmaus, and lastly the gathering of the apostles in Jerusalem in the late evening. St John tells of Mary Magdalene, Peter and John at the tomb, of the disciples assembled in the upper room, and of Thomas. They have recorded who were the witnesses of the Resurrection and what they saw and heard.

There is good reason why the last chapters of all the Gospels are written in the same style. Every Christian person has to become himself a witness of the Resurrection. Those described by the evangelists were the first, who should be followed by a host of others, who know out of their individual experience that Christ is risen. Some people would like to think: we need a definite statement of what actually happened, then we shall believe. Yet belief does not come through statements of this kind, which can be dissected at will by critics. The cloud of witnesses, of those who know, carry the fact of the Resurrection into human minds and hearts. No one can find this knowledge through historical proof or through the conviction of another. Each one has to see the fact for himself, become a witness, out of that which he has thought, felt and understood, of Christ's deed of death and life.

The Resurrection was an event which changed the history of the world. It dawned like a great sunrise of the Spirit's light and none of the witnesses was able to see the whole. Each of them caught a glimpse through the window of his heart's consciousness of a happening which was beyond all description. When we read the Gospels, we are able to look through the eyes and hear with the ears of one after another of the men and women who experienced the first day of Easter. In so doing, our hearts may begin to apprehend something of that which they saw in a glimpse. What they knew may start to kindle knowledge in ourselves.

The stories in all the Gospels have one feature in common. They mark clearly the time at which each experience took place. They point to a transition from what was seen at dawn, later on the same day, and still later at other times. A second common feature is the distinction between what the women experienced and the men. The women all received a different kind of revelation from that which came to the disciples. What is said in the four Gospels may be so read that these distinctions of time and persons illumine our outlook on to the world event which all the witnesses beheld.

In the earliest light of the morning the one fact stood revealed which could be seen with ordinary sight by everyone, the empty tomb. All the women, described by the four evangelists, the two disciples mentioned by St John, the soldiers whose history is recorded by St Matthew, saw that the stone was rolled away and the tomb was bare of all but the linen clothes in which the body had been shrouded. A modern writer on the subject has remarked that the empty tomb is the single fact in the history of Jesus Christ upon which everyone present at the time agreed and which has never been disputed since. St Matthew says that the Jewish priests bribed the soldiers to spread the news that the body had been stolen, but even they accepted without question the fact that the tomb was empty. Negative as the fact is, nevertheless it has great significance. Spiritual insight was and is now necessary to perceive that Christ rose again. Yet a sign of this great spiritual event was actually impressed into the material, physical layer of existence, in a form such that people with their ordinary eyes, whether they were interested or not, whether they believed or not, could see it. This sign was the empty tomb. Even a materialist can accept it without argument. But those who rely on material evidence and trust to earth-bound faculties, will not get beyond this negative fact. They continue to stand before the picture of the empty tomb, as before a sphinx with an unanswerable question. They only hear the words: He is not here.

When the two Marys, of whom St Matthew speaks, came to the sepulchre, they saw the stone rolled from the mouth of the cave and the soldiers, who had been put on guard, lying in a dead faint overwhelmed by fear. Being innocent women, intent upon a good task, they were not overcome by what they saw behind the prostrate soldiers. In the light of the dawn, while the ground was still shuddering with the tremors of the great earthquake that had just passed, they beheld an angel of the Lord. He was sitting upon the stone, which he had rolled back from the door of the tomb. The women perceived that not only His disciples and friends, the soldiers and His enemies, were involved in this great event, but that a host of divine beings, mostly beyond the range of their sight, were taking part. They saw that this angel was one from the hierarchies of the Heavens, they felt the trembling of the ground as the sign that other unseen powers were with and around him. They were dimly aware that a divine deed, at which all the beings of God were assisting, was being performed on the earth, from which the heavenly powers had so long been distant. The appearance of the angel was such that gazing on him was like trying to look at lightning. He was clad in white as glittering and pure as snow. The angel spoke as someone would to his friends, saying that he knew for whom they searched, but that He was not there, He was risen. They were in that moment as people accepted into the community of the angels, made their companions out of their common care and longing for Christ.

On that early Easter morning the women had a glimpse into the cosmic event which the Resurrection was in truth. The angel who shook the ground at the earthquake was one of the heavenly host who, as the helpers of the Son-god, had at the beginning created the world. As a consequence of the fall of Man into the power of Evil, the divine beings had withdrawn to a distance. But the Son of God had descended into the world from which they had departed. He had penetrated into the realm of death, from which He had risen again. At His rising the other sons of God came to meet Him. The process of a new creation, which is still unfinished, began in the hour of resurrection, when the ground trembled at the coming of Him, whose light shone triumphant, brighter even than the countenance of the angel that was as lightning.

When the women turned away from the tomb, to take the message of the angel to the apostles, they met Jesus. Their hearts were in a tumult of fear and joy after their experience at the tomb. When they saw Him, they became quiet and fell into a deep mood of worship. It is strange that He was in that moment familiar to the women, wrapping them in the peace of His accustomed presence. No other story of Easter tells of His appearance in such a manner. It was very early in the day, the women were deeply shaken by the grief of Good Friday, by anxious hope and by the meeting with the angel. One may imagine that when they met Jesus they had come into the state of mind in which visions are easily seen. He was present with them in reality, but His appearance was clothed in that which they remembered. They did not see His risen form, as others were to do later, but they met Him in a soul-experience, where His real presence was mirrored in their memories.

In scenes from the other Gospels, one may notice again and again that the women who went at dawn to the garden where the tomb lay were in a state of consciousness in which visions might easily appear to them. The experiences which the men had at a later time, when they were gathered together within doors, were of another character. They met Him in a sphere in which earthly facts are perceived. They could be convinced that the Risen One came to them, not in the pictures of dreams or visions, but in actual fact. Nevertheless, the women were the first to meet Him. St Matthew's Gospel closes with the scene in which the apostles met Christ on the mountain, as He had foretold through the women. The many meetings He had with them in the forty days following the first Easter Sunday are gathered into one picture, which also includes a suggestion of the Ascension. The mountain in Galilee represents the sphere of soul in which they met Him, the uplifted mood of their hearts. In Galilee they had first become disciples, and the force of this early devotion rose up again within them, that they might receive the new commission as apostles. Not an outer landscape is meant, but the inner state of soul, in which they were present in the company of the Risen One. His power streamed into them, His light gave them new life of spirit, and His words sent them out into the future as the bearers of Christianity.

Three women, says St Mark, went at dawn to the tomb. They found the stone rolled away and the place empty. There appeared to them a young man in a white vestment, who told them that

Christ had risen. Like the two women of whom St Matthew tells, they looked in a flash beyond the sphere of humankind into the world of beings greater than men, whose existence is not material. They saw a youthful form, but he whom they gazed upon was not one from their own world. He was a being so close to Jesus Christ that he was a part of His nature. So it came about that he wore the semblance of a man, for he had partaken of the incarnation of Christ in Jesus. Nevertheless, he was not himself the Risen One. Through crucifixion and death the being of Jesus Christ had dissolved from the whole into parts. The body of Jesus had been taken by the earth. His Spirit, which was His essential self, entered the struggle with death and overcame it. Another part of His being watched over Him from above. Strong with the pure strength of the virgin forces of the universe, those powers of creation which had not yet been absorbed into material existence, the cosmic being, who had accompanied Him from Heaven to earth, stood before the women in the shadow of the tomb. They beheld the youth, like a radiant token of the world's power of renewal. They saw the tomb in the background, a symbol of the dead and empty past, and in the foreground the shining young man in the priestly vestment, proclaiming to them the good news of resurrection. In the early years of Christianity, when the Christians painted the walls of the catacombs in Rome, one of their favourite pictures most often repeated was that of a beautiful youth. They loved more than any other this way of representing Christ. He has brought us the new birth, has given us the source of life from Heaven, is the thought behind such paintings. They express what the three women, spoken of by St Mark, saw at the tomb when they beheld on Easter morning the beautiful youth, the heavenly One, whose appearance and whose words opened their eyes to the world event of the Resurrection.

Very early in the morning, tells St Luke, women went with spices to the tomb. Three women and a small crowd of others, says this evangelist, in whose Gospel the words "and others" are added on every occasion, that no one should be excluded. Again, the stone was rolled away and the tomb empty. Two powerful figures of men stood near, clad in a brightness like that of lightning, so dazzling that the women bowed to the ground. They told them that He had risen, as He had already foretold many times. The women ran to tell the disciples, and Peter came to see. He found the tomb and the empty cloths, but he saw no shining figures. In the light of the dawn the women, like those described by St Mark, had seen further into what was happening in the act of resurrection than he could see, coming later in a less uplifted mood. They had beheld face to face the two beings who were so close to Christ that they stood sentinel at the place where His body had been laid. Who were they? It happens to everyone, in the process of death, that his being is dispersed into its parts. The organism of life, separating from the corpse, follows the living soul out into the universe. Those three portions of man's nature, the physical, the living and the soul parts, which have been locked together for a lifetime, are pulled apart at death. The earth takes the body, and the spaces of the universe receive what was life and soul. So it was also with Jesus Christ, though that which had been His life and His soul was as much more powerful and light-filled than that which proceeds from a human being as His body was more purified. These two parts of His being appeared to the women of whom St Luke tells. Bright as angels, but human in form, these two prophetic figures represent those portions of His being that had been the vessels of His Spirit.

Later in the same day, says St Luke, two disciples were walking in the glare of noon to a village beyond Jerusalem. They were talking in bewilderment of what had happened. A stranger joined them, who to their amazement understood better than they what had come to pass. In the evening at the meal, He blessed their bread, and they saw that He whom they held to be a stranger was the One for whom their hearts were yearning. They returned in haste to Jerusalem and found the other disciples gathered together in an upper room. By that time it was night, and Peter had already told the others how he had seen the Risen One, though where and how is not said. Then, about midnight, for so it must have been, He was in their midst, speaking the blessing: Peace be unto you. They all knew Him at once, but they were in doubt as to whether they were seeing only His dead ghost. Thereupon He showed them His hands and His side and took the fish and honey they offered, eating it before their eyes. In that hour they perceived that He was present in a physical sense, that He was showing them His mastery over the nature of matter. They realised that He had not departed into another world, but had united His existence, in a way they could not yet grasp, with human life on earth. The latter part of this scene does not represent one appearance of the Risen Christ on one night, but it indicates the period of continual communion between Him and the apostles, which lasted from Easter Sunday until Ascension Day. The teaching He gave to them during these days of resurrection is summarised as if it were a parting message. St Luke describes the meeting of the Risen One with the apostles as if it were a small seed, the sprouting and growing of which is not included in the Gospel. The seed was to grow later, after Whitsun, when those who had hidden so long in a secret place became the first messengers of Christianity.

In St John's Gospel the distinct character of the appearances seen by the women and the men is still clearer. The times of day are so stressed that the event of the Resurrections begins to emerge before the eyes of the reader as a process which took a definite number of hours and days to accomplish. The women saw with visionary sight what had happened at the early stage of the process, and the men were able to behold what came afterwards. In all the Gospels we find that the women experienced what they saw early in the morning out in the garden where the tomb lay. The apostles, except those who walked to Emmaus, met the Risen One in the evening within doors, where they had withdrawn into a place of safety. Their eyes were opened by spiritual insight, when they beheld Him, to perceive that He stood before them in a body of a new kind. The women, within whom a different power of sight was awakened, did not penetrate to this knowledge.

St John tells of only one woman who came to the tomb in the morning, Mary Magdalene. She found it empty and called two disciples to the place. They saw the empty tomb and went again. One of them apprehended at once the true idea of the Resurrection when he perceived the dark void where the body had lain. Mary, through her tears, saw two angels standing in the tomb. The purifying effect of her grief had so changed her sight that she could look into the sphere of the angels. Turning round, she saw next the Risen One Himself, seeming to be the gardener come to tend the newly sprouting plants. But when He spoke her name she knew Him. Her eyes saw Him, her ears heard Him, but she was forbidden to touch Him with her hands. The body which He brought out of death was not yet born into that layer of existence at which it could be reached by the sense of touch. Mary was looking into the sphere where the forces of life live and weave, where the angels dwell. There she saw her Lord, risen from death but not yet master of the realm where the forces of existence condense into matter.

The words He spoke to Mary give a glimpse into the mysterious process of the Resurrection. On the same day, in the evening, He entered the room where the disciples were gathered, and they saw Him in their midst, showing them the marks of the wounds on hands and side. They beheld the risen body born out of death, perfected now in a form that could be seen, but also touched. Thomas, the apostle who was not present on the first evening, declared that he could not believe unless he might touch the wounds. One week later he was with the others when the Risen One came again. On Easter morning, Mary had been told "Touch me not". Now Thomas was invited to stretch out his hands to feel the wounds. In this manner the words of the Gospel call us to contemplate the hidden process by which the new body of the Risen One grew into the spiritual, yet physical form which was made known to the apostles. The risen body was the token by which they recognised that Christ had overcome the power of death within the existence of the earth, and therewith saved the souls of human beings from its sting. In the distant future, those who follow Him will grow into a new state, when their bodies will become like His risen body. By virtue of this deed, the human form divine will not be lost at the world's end but will become a living temple for the redeemed souls of men. The way of evolution towards this end is the path of salvation. Christ at His resurrection united His being with the destiny of Mankind, that He might become Himself the way by which human souls may attain their resurrection. During the time in which He lived with the apostles in the days of Easter, the revelation of this truth was made known to them. In their hearts dawned slowly the understanding that His resurrection was to be the source of man's future and their hope of salvation. They could say with Thomas: My Lord and my God.

The event of the Resurrection is described in the Gospels through the eyes of a few witnesses. In contemplation of these stories, we may enter into what they experienced and look through what they saw to the great dawn of Christ's light upon earth. So we may grow in understanding that we may find the fact of the Resurrection present in our inner experience and in the life of the world around us. We may join the crowd of witnesses, that follow the women, standing by the empty tomb, and the apostles gathered together behind closed doors.

THE DAYS OF RESURRECTION

When the spring arrives, when the leaves come out on the trees and the first flowers can be found in garden and hedgerow, the world around, that has been bare and dark during the winter, grows beautiful again. The season of flowering has come, bringing joy to the beholder. The summer never quite satisfies the expectation of the spring. How delicate and light-filled is the green-gold of the half-grown, early leaves. When summer has fully come, they are bigger and coarser and their green has thickened. Their beauty has not increased, it has declined. In springtime the leaves are flower-like, and the blossoms are beings of pure colour only just held in material shape by the petals. The loveliness of spring is that of flowering.

No creatures of the earth show their true, spiritual nature so clearly and directly as do the plants in blossom. A stone, even the most beautifully-shaped crystal, is only a memory of its true nature. An animal shows hints of its spiritual being but in its earthbound form is a creature under a spell, unable to be itself. How deeply does insight need to penetrate the heart of a fellow human being to perceive something of what truly lives within him. But the flowers are in their whole appearance a clear reflection of what they are in the Divine World under the eyes of God. In springtime we are united in experience with the beings of God, when we behold their beauty. The charm of this season lies in this, that the earthly world is then most transparent for the Divine World. With the coming of summer, the plants lost part of this transparency. The heaviness of earth begins to weigh them down, to make the light which they have received from above dense with the darkness from below.

During the days of resurrection, when the apostles lived in the presence of the Risen One, they experienced a springtime of the Spirit. Outwardly they were in hiding from the rulers of the Jews, who wished to persecute them. They gathered together in a place of sanctuary, which was most probably the upper room where the Last Supper had been held. In the house of the much respected order of the Essenes, they could remain outwardly undisturbed. In the room which had, through all that had taken place there, become their temple, they lived between Easter and Ascension. They were constantly aware that the Risen One was of their company. The light and power of His resurrection shone upon and around them. That which the Transfiguration had shown prophetically to a few of them for a moment became the daily experience of the whole community of the apostles.

They saw their Master as they had never been able to see Him before. The body of Jesus had hidden Him from their sight. The body of the resurrection revealed to them His godhood. Thomas, when he realised at whom he was gazing, whose wounds it was he wished to touch, said: "my Lord and my God" (St John, ch. 20, v. 28). He and the others saw with their own power of insight that they were beholding the Son of God. Nor was this the experience only of a moment. For the forty days of Easter they dwelt in His presence and they received from Him the wisdom of the world of God from which He had come. The divine mysteries of the universe that are indicated in symbols by the patterns traced in the shining stars across the Heavens appeared to them as He spoke. They felt as an inner, spiritual experience what the flowers feel when the sunlight falls upon them. They felt shining into their innermost being in the light of truth all that the genius of the sun knows of the World-all. That which streamed forth from the Risen One was the divine wisdom weaving in the world-light. They likewise felt themselves penetrated into the depths of the heart by the power of the world-warmth. The sunbeams, that cause the flowers to blossom and the bees to hum, carry the outer warmth of the sun to earth. The Risen One brought the inner warmth to the apostles, and it became in them the power of love. The quickening might of the heart's power of love entered into them and began to transform them from within. The days of resurrection were a time of communion between the Son of God and the sons of men, when He poured His divine gifts of light and love into their souls.

After forty days this time came to an end. Why the beauty of the springtime ceases can be understood through what follows in the summer. The blossoms must fade after a while, because the plant is bringing forth the seed from within the flower's cup. The season of fruiting follows the flowering in the natural rhythm of the plant's existence. The earthly nature is stronger in the fruit, the heavenly is more apparent in the flower. Yet the fruit contains the seed of the new growth. The flower cannot go further. It must fade for the sake of what is to come. So it was in the days of the resurrection. The flowering of the Risen One's presence had to change into fruiting. If the springtime had not ended, Christ's deed of death and resurrection could not have borne fruit on the earth. The hearts of the apostles, that had been open to Him like flowers to the sun, were the place where the new seed had to be formed. As a fruit puts flesh and rind round the seed-chambers at its core, so the earthly being of the apostles had to become the outer covering for the new seeds of the Spirit quickened within them by the world-light and the world-warmth of the spiritual Sun. This could only happen when the immediate, visible presence of the Risen One was withdrawn, that the hearts of the apostles might no longer be absorbed entirely in what shone upon them from without, but that, looking within, they might find the seed entrusted to their care. The Ascension, ending the forty days of resurrection, brought them a grievous loss, but it gave them the opportunity to find in themselves the meaning of their earthly life. To cherish and tend the seed of the Spirit became their task.

That which was planted first in the apostles is the seed given to every human soul by the deed of Christ. We all partake in the new beginning of human life on earth, which is the gift of the resurrection. Salvation does not mean the ending of all the troubles and struggles of existence: it has another meaning, which is that the great tribulation of the life on earth becomes a way of progress towards the new manhood of Man. Christ said to the apostles, He says to all human souls who follow Him: "I am the way, the truth and the life" (St John, ch. 14, v. 6). That is to say: I am the way through the struggle of earthly life to the ideal of new manhood. I am the truth, who brings to you from the Divine World, whose very substance is truth, the new pattern of Man. When this shall become real in you, then you will find the truth in yourselves. I am the life which you will find at the end of the way, when in your true, resurrected being you will enter into the life of the Divine World. I am the way, the light upon the way, and the way's end and purpose. So speaks the Risen One to those who understand His revelation.

When we look into the world around us and wonder at the beauty of creation in the spring, we see the revelation of God. His true presence, not seen in reflection but face to face, is in the World of Spirit. Man finds his place of growth and development in the world of reflection, that is to say of the earth, as long as his new manhood is not yet matured. Christ leads him on the way through earthly life and, when all is fulfilled, He will take him, made true Man in the Spirit, into the presence of the Father-god. Then Man will be received into the divine worlds of life, where he will find true existence.

ASCENSION

ASCENSION

This festival is part of the cycle of Easter. It follows forty days after the beginning of the time of resurrection. The date changes in the calendar each year with that of Easter, but Ascension Day always falls on a Thursday. Ten days later comes Whitsunday, with which the short season of Ascension closes. Few festivals present such a problem for people today as this, which may account for the fact that it is not so generally celebrated as Easter and Whitsuntide. Nevertheless in the Christian cycle of festivals it is an essential part of the experience leading from the one to the other. Looking back to the events described in the Gospels, Ascension commemorates the close of the days of resurrection, during which the apostles lived in the immediate presence of the Risen One. They saw Him received out of their sight into the clouds. It marks the beginning of a fresh phase in the process of resurrection, the reunion of Christ with the realms of the Father. The life of Christianity today still flows from this event, as the water of a stream continually wells up from its source. For this reason it is so important to understand its significance anew in the present time.

Ascension falls when the season of blossoming comes to the full. Trees and plants, stirring upwards in growth, have been touched by the warmth and light from above and show forth the blessing of the Heavens in the colour and scent of blossoms. The whole of Nature reaches upwards towards the heights. The feeling and longing of human souls strives upward in unison with plant and blossom, seeking the touch of the world-warmth from the sun. The mood of Ascension arises spontaneously in the realms of the plants, among the animals and in the souls of human beings. However earthbound our interests at other seasons, at this time we naturally become aware of the heights, living in reality not quite on the earth but absorbed by what is happening in the regions of the air. The light comes towards us in the weaving air and we yearn to fill ourselves with the treasure of its warmth, to enjoy the scintillations of colour and catch the drifting scents. Our hearts turn heavenward in the natural mood of early summer.

The Ascension of Christ is the returning of Him who had descended to earth, overcome death, risen again to life, into the kingdoms of the Father. His reaching heavenward has left an impress on our mood and that of Nature at this festival. But when we look upwards today, what kind of experience does this mean? What is our idea of the Heavens? It must sadly be admitted that looking upward means for many people today looking into vagueness. The stars in their constellations are spread out over the night sky and the planets tread the ordered measure of their courses among them. Is this the painted ceiling of our world? Are the points of light in the distance immense worlds of their own, before which our small world appears insignificant and puny? Do the stars, to which we look up, speak of a soulless, heartless universe, a mechanical contrivance of forces? Points of view such as these will be the only ones understandable to people whose minds are not willing to contemplate the existence of beings, invisible and spiritual in their nature, who direct the life of the universe. Ascension is the festival of the angels, archangels and all the company of Heaven. Its meaning is of the vaguest if they are ignored. When they appear within the picture of Christianity, this festival comes into its own and is filled with significance.

The shining points of the stars are indications of worlds that are hidden from our earthly eyes. Sometimes, going down a dark road at night, by a trick of illumination, one can see the eyes of an animal gleaming, while the body is hidden in the darkness. The stars are eyes shining in the night, while the beings behind them are hidden from our sight, but not from the vision of our minds. Beings of nine ranks or hierarchies inhabit the worlds, of which the stars are the sign. They maintain and order the universe, to which our earth also belongs, with their influences.

They are all members of God's being, portions of His existence, contemplating His thoughts, living by His will. They differ in the order of their evolution, in the power of their influence, and in the universal functions they fulfil. The Being of God is manifoldness in unity, is worlds of Spirit united in the universal Divine. Our human comprehension is easily overwhelmed before such a conception. We have the means of grasping it, however, in its reflection in ourselves. We are made in the image of God in the sense that we also are manifold and yet one. Take, for instance, the internal organs in the human body. They each have their own being and state of existence, yet in community with one another their functioning is our life. Their manifoldness contributes to our sense of being one.

Behind the universe of the stars, which is the visible portion of God's dwelling, are living, moving beings of nine divine orders. They are creatures of life, soul and spirit. They look with care and a desire to heal towards the children of Mankind who dwell on the earth. The universe is anything but soulless. It is filled with the heart-forces of the hierarchies, that stream and weave through the world. The heart of Man is narrow and personal compared with the heart of the world, that is of God, but it can open itself to the divine light and warmth as flowers open their sunlike blossoms to the sun.

Before He came down to earth, Christ dwelt in the world of the Father-god as the companion of the divine beings of the nine hierarchies. When He left the Heavens and descended into human form, they lost His presence and saw Him depart into the distant, mysterious world of earth. They knew nothing of death from their own experience. They saw from afar the dark, unknown power which had the earth in its grip, that had made of it a lost godforsaken world. Christ went from them and they could only find Him afar by looking downward into the depths. He performed the deed of death and life on Golgotha, the act done by the Son of God in the lost world. All the hierarchies of Heaven looked on in wonder at this deed. They understood that, although it was performed among people on earth, it was of significance for the whole universe. Nevertheless, the Risen One revealed Himself to human beings earlier than to the heavenly host. He taught the apostles to contemplate and experience the fact of resurrection before He showed it to them. The change in the course of evolution which then began was initiated on earth and was made known first to human souls, though their understanding was too limited to grasp what they perceived. Afterwards, at a later stage, the Risen One proclaimed the resurrection to the company of Heaven. This was done at the Ascension.

The apostles seemed to behold Him received into the clouds, passing out of their sight. What happened then was an expansion of Christ's being into the universe. For forty days He had lived in the concentrated form of the risen body, that was perceptible and tangible to the apostles. Concentration then changed into expansion. The universe received the Risen One. The Heavens saw Him come into the heights, expanding His being into the universal proportions which are its true form. He became too vast for the sight of the apostles, which could not reach to the Heavens. He seemed to vanish into the distance, because His being reached beyond their limits. They thought to lose Him in the present, because He had grown to fill the cycles of Time. The sons of God in their nine hierarchies received Him back into their community. They found again the One who had gone into the far country.

They heard from Him the secret of that which had been beyond their experience. They received the knowledge of death and of how life had been brought out of death. The vision of the Heavens was increased and enriched with the new treasure Christ had won out of the struggle with evil and death in the world, so long godforsaken, of the earth. The universe of God held within itself the wisdom of creation, the mystery of the world-creating Word that flows from the divine silence. Now, at Ascension, the wisdom of resurrection, that had been brought forth in the depths, was made known in the heights. The company of Heaven beheld the new mystery that had been brought forth among people on earth, of life born out of death.

At the Ascension the Son of God was welcomed back into the Father's house in the Heavens. This was no loss for the world of earth. At the resurrection Christ united Himself with this world and with the future history of Mankind. He became its presiding Spirit, its genius. He has made it His abode, the place of His working, of His labour for the resurrection of Man. His Ascension to the Heavens is the return of the lost world of the earth into the community of the stars. Since that time the life of this planet is renewed with the heavenly forces that stream earthward. A picture among those of the Old Testament is a prophecy of the Ascension. Jacob dreamed that he saw a ladder set between earth and Heaven, on which the angels of God went up and down. When the risen Christ returned to the universe, He set up the golden ladder between two worlds. He dwells with us on earth and reaches with His Spirit into the divine presence of the Father in the Heavens. He is in Himself the fulfilment of the old prophecy of the ladder, for through Him Mankind is brought near again to the angels, archangels and all the company of Heaven.

At Ascension we see with our inner eyes Christ in His place in the universe, we glimpse His significance for the whole cosmos. This vision should make us aware that Man is likewise a creature of the universe, that his salvation is the concern of all the sons of God, who have the stars for their habitation. Today it is a difficult matter to contemplate the true dignity of Man as it lives in the thought of God. The courage for great aims and high endeavour does not come easily to us. It is easier and more comfortable to think of our human nature as poor and weak, of ourselves as too insignificant to be expected to fill an important place in the universe. Nevertheless, Christ has taken on the form of a man. His risen body has the pattern of the human form divine and today, when He comes to meet us along the road of life, another, transfigured human being stands before us. As He has ascended so, in the fullness of time, Man, transfigured into the image of Christ, will ascend. The angels, archangels and the company of Heaven wait for their youngest brother who has taken so long to complete his earthly task, to ascend into their fellowship. Christ goes with divine patience through the evolution of Mankind, helping human souls along the way that leads to ascension. He reminds us of the true ideal of Man which we could not retain by our own strength.

In the present age an event takes place in the history of Christ that mirrors back again what happened at the Ascension. At that time He passed out of the apostles' range of vision and expanded into His universal godhood. Today He can so far concentrate His being into visible form that He can be seen from time to time by people in whom the mind's power of vision has been intensified for a few moments. This can most readily happen to those who are for a while under great stress that their customary mode of consciousness is changed. He takes on an appearance condensed from the life-forces that weave round and into the earth. The clouds are the clearest manifestation of this kind of force, since all their existence and behaviour is directed by them. So it comes about that this form of Christ-revelation is called the "coming in the clouds". Those who from time to time meet Him face to face in this manner see another human being before them. They see the Son of God, who has taken on and retained manhood. Their eyes are opened for the vision of what has still to be evolved in Mankind on earth if Man is to fulfil the destiny to which he is called by God. The revelation of Christ is the summons to human souls to seek the way that leads to the ascension into the company of Heaven.

WHITSUNTIDE

WHITSUNTIDE

Ascensiontide ends with the festival of Whitsun. In one sense the Easter cycle of festivals has its conclusion in this one, which celebrates the descent of the Holy Spirit. In another sense it is the beginning of a new series of festivals, somewhat different in character from those that precede it. We contemplate in those that follow one another from Advent to Whitsuntide the history of Christ becoming Man, of the divine deed performed on earth. Then come the festivals that belong to the summer months, beginning with Whitsuntide and continuing with St John's tide and Michaelmas. They are filled with another revelation, that of Christ's working within Mankind, of the slow transformation of Man into His image. We contemplate at this season that which has not yet been achieved but which belongs to the present and future history of our world. Whitsuntide completes Easter and at the same time initiates the chain of festivals in the summer half of the year.

Its date depends on that of Easter. In the course of the seasons it stands on the threshold between spring and summer. The time of flowering has come in Nature but the seeding process is already beginning. The world-warmth of the sun, who is now reaching the height of his course through the sky, quickens the swelling seeds. As summer approaches, it often happens that there are thunderstorms from time to time. Thunder rolls through the clouds, lightning-flashes strike through the air and the sky is troubled with the upheaval of storm. When this happens it brings a violent change in the atmosphere. The conditions over a part of the earth's surface alter suddenly. This is due to the breaking in of forces from beyond the mantle of the atmosphere, which is wrapped round the earth. Spiritual forces of life from the world's heights cut their way downwards, taking, in the region of the clouds, the appearance of rolling thunder, rushing wind and the flash of lightning. Thunderstorms clear the air, wash the world clean and bring a fresh impulse of life from above. The true heaven-sent storms have this effect. Nowadays another kind of stormy weather often afflicts us. The clouds hang low over the land, they move onwards, but for long periods they neither break in a downpour nor dissolve into the upper air. They seem to be moving round and round over a stretch of country, shutting off the sun. A kind of false storm exists, which accumulates in the upper air through that which rises up from the sphere of human life. It is no mere fancy to suppose that the disbelief in the Divine World and the feelings arising therefrom befog the atmosphere and produce false storm-clouds.

The idea of the thunderstorm is the clue to the description we read in the Acts of the Apostles of the descent of the Holy Spirit. The apostles and Mary were gathered together in the upper room. The thunder of a rushing, mighty wind was heard. Flames of lightning flashed down on the heads of each one. A spiritual thunderstorm took place, by which a fresh impulse of the Spirit penetrated the hearts and souls of the apostles and Mary. Though the storm was not physical but spiritual, the process which happened followed the same pattern as that of an outer burst of thunder. The power of the Holy Spirit came down from the heights of the Divine World into the sphere of the earth and lighted an inner flame within the souls of men. The indwelling power of the Spirit was born into Mankind.

The Holy Spirit was known before this event, but in a different manner. A divine force working from outside the soul, from the world beyond the earthly, giving inspiration, directing certain chosen people in their life-work, had been known to those who lived before the coming of Christ. Yet the real presence of the divine Being was hidden in the Heavens. In those times the Spirit which entered most immediately into human souls was the genius of the tribe or race. Each tribal group was led by a folk-spirit, to whom the people looked as the nearest, most accessible portion of the Godhead. The old Hebrew people addressed Jehovah as the "God of Israel". Other races called upon their own gods. The distinction between religions was racial and tribal. Each religion had its portion of divine wisdom and revealed a part of the universal Being of God. It would be true to say that then, before the life of Christ on earth, the whole picture of God was spread out over the peoples of the world on the face of the earth. In the mystery-temples in the various lands where the different religions were cultivated, separate portions of God's revelation of Himself were known and worshipped. Had anyone then desired to know the whole picture, he would have had to become a pilgrim journeying from land to land, entering one mystery-temple after another, knowing one religion after another. Then he would have gathered together the different portions of the revelation of God's universal being. What he would have gathered in each experience would have been manifested through the genius or god of the particular race. Hidden behind the gods who guided the various nations, withdrawn within the Divine World, the Holy Spirit lived, moved and had His mysterious being.

The Holy Spirit is the same for all peoples over the face of the earth. His descent among Mankind has changed the nature of religion. Christianity is not the worship of one race of people. Everyone, to whatever nation he belongs, can find Christianity and it will be as true for him as for someone from another race. In some parts of the world today the old forms of religion that are bound to nation and tribe still persist. Those people born in such countries will have a more difficult access to Christianity than those who are, for instance, born into European nations. Nevertheless, the fact is not altered that Christianity is not, as previous religions have been, a national faith, under the leadership of the tribal god. It is the faith for Mankind, in which earlier religions find their fulfilment. They were all, to whatever race they belonged, preparing for the coming of the Son of God. The people of Israel called Him, who was to come, the Messiah. Their particular task of preparation was to provide the human body in which His Spirit could dwell. Other races of people before His coming had different missions, but they all awaited Him, though they called Him by different names. Their worship prophesied His descent to earth as truly as the preaching of the prophets in the Old Testament. The prologue to St John's Gospel, which is a psalm about the creation of the world, could not have been written without the Greek philosophy which went before. Philosophy for the Greeks was the divine wisdom revealed to human thinking and had its origin in the ancient mystery-cults. The Greeks had their particular task in preparing the thought with which to understand His coming.

The Holy Spirit is the Spirit of Mankind. After the gift of the inner flame to the apostles, Christianity began to become a religion. Under the inspiration of the Holy Spirit it could be proclaimed to all peoples, each with their own kind of understanding, and could be received as the faith which is beyond distinctions of race. A reading of the stories in the Gospels shows us how different was Jesus Christ from the honoured and well-known figures of the prophets of the Old Testament. The birth of Jesus was prepared by the Holy Spirit and not by the guiding spirit of the people of Israel, under whom all the great Hebrew leaders had been born. Jesus was in a spiritual sense the Child of Mankind. When the baptism in Jordan took place, the Spirit descended from Heaven to dwell within the earthly sheath of Jesus. A being inspired by the universal Spirit of God was so unknown that the people around were continually puzzled by the riddle of who He could be in reality. They understood John the Baptist, for he truly represented the ancient tradition of Israel. But when asked if he were the promised Messiah he denied it and pointed to the mysterious, quiet figure of the unknown one, and said: "Behold the Lamb of God." In the scenes from the first chapter of St John's Gospel we can observe how mysterious and incomprehensible was the One upon whom the Spirit of all Mankind rested.

In our present time the task is still unfinished of receiving into our understanding the Holy Spirit, who belongs to all Mankind. The expression "Mankind" is still vague in meaning, for we are uncertain as to what the true quality of our humanity should be. The Holy Spirit leads us towards the knowledge of what Man shall become in Christ, that he may become Man in truth. Although He is the Spirit of all Mankind, His dwelling is the single human heart. In the Acts of the Apostles, where the descent of the Spirit in the thunderstorm is described, we read that the apostles were together as they had been in the time when their Master was present. As a community they had all passed through the experience of following Jesus Christ along the way of His earthly life, of living through the time of Golgotha, of finding Him again in His risen form. Through the days of resurrection they had shared His presence, His instruction and His inspiration, which had taken hold of their hearts and penetrated into the core of their being. At the Ascension they had seen Him expand into the distances of space and time beyond their sight. A common longing to find His presence again filled all their souls. Shared experience and common longing welded them into a community of the most intense kind on the morning of Pentecost. They were of one heart and mind. The spiritual thunderstorm began and the flames entered into them. The knowledge of Christ lighted up in their hearts. They found Him again, but in so different a manner. An inner presence within each one, an enlightened consciousness, the power to speak of what they knew, revealed to the apostles the indwelling of the Spirit.

Each received the same Spirit, but each discovered the flame within his own single heart. True individuality in the spiritual life comes from the Holy Spirit. Yet His indwelling power which allows each human soul to know himself in a spiritual sense is that which enlightens us with an understanding for our humanity, with the knowledge of Mankind as a whole. That which is most individual and lives most intensely in our inward depths is likewise that which we have in common with other human souls, which enables us to understand that we are united in Mankind. The apostles received, each one into his single heart, the light-giving flame of the Spirit. They were each able to keep the gift, to enshrine it in their inner being, to preserve the living and working power, by the strength of their community. The gift was sent out of the Divine World. The hearts of the apostles formed together the chalice into which it was poured and which was able to hold and keep what was given. They received on behalf of all Mankind that which can dwell in each single heart.

The Holy Spirit works as the power of enlightenment. Until they were endowed with this gift the apostles were unable to think and know what they had experienced of Christ. Once they were enlightened, they could proclaim Christianity to the people around them. They had the strength and knowledge to found the Christian Church. Since that time the enlightening power of the Spirit is found within all human souls, if they wish to seek it and give it the opportunity of expression. The way in which the voice of enlightenment speaks evolves from age to age. In our time, it no longer speaks from outside giving directions and instructions, which was the manner in which the first apostles heard it. Many stories in the book of their Acts record conversations with the Holy Spirit of such a kind. Today the Spirit speaks within, in our human power of thinking, when by our inner effort we lift our thinking out of earthbound limits towards the sphere of true spiritual ideas. The voice speaks in the ideals that are born in truth and in spirit within our hearts. The power of enlightenment grows stronger from age to age. The gift of Whitsuntide is given again in our own age, if we know how to accept and comprehend it.

The Holy Spirit works to heal the nature of Man from within. All that the sickness of sin has done to unfit human nature for the Spirit, to spoil the image of God within us, needs healing. The being of God has looked upon the children of men, has seen their infirmity and the danger that they will be destroyed in death. Out of the divine will to heal, the Father in the Heavens has poured forth the Spirit through Christ into human souls. The healing Spirit is the gift of God given out of the wealth of the Divine World to heal the poverty, weakness and sinfulness of people on earth. The ideal of man for the future, the prophecy of the resurrected nature, is given by the risen Christ. The power of healing through which human souls can grow and become in the image of the Christian ideal is given by the Spirit who brings both enlightenment and healing. We celebrate at Whitsuntide the power dwelling within us to become Christian.

THE TRINITY

When Whitsuntide has come and gone, the cycle is complete of the festivals which are related to the incarnation, death and resurrection of Christ. When we look back upon the picture made by the whole sequence, recognising that His was the deed of God performed among men, we realise that it was as significant for the dwellers in the Heavens as it is for the inhabitants of the earth. When we begin to ponder its heavenly aspect, we encounter the idea of God, which has been born in human minds through Christianity. We contemplate the mystery of the Trinity. Today this idea has become a problem for many people, for in the course of centuries it has been made into a point of doctrine calling for explanation. In reality it should be now, as in early times, an idea that can be seen in the light of its own truth. When so seen, it is a source of insight into the meaning of Christ's deed for the Divine World, from which He descended into the realm of earth.

To know the Godhead in the three aspects, the Father, the Son and the Holy Spirit, is not a matter of teaching that can be learnt, but of the mind's power of vision. We are not any of us able to have insight of this nature at all stages of our lifetime. We are incapable of it in childhood, but we develop the necessary powers of mind in the course of the changes that take place in a child as he grows up to be a youth. In other words, insight into the threefold nature of God is possible to all human souls when they have acquired the faculties proper to grown-up people. Little children are by nature full of faith in God and willing to see His handiwork in the abundant world around them. Older people may often learn from them such natural confidence in what is divine. It may disappear later, as the soul grows further into the body and the being of the child descends deeper into existence on earth. Nevertheless, most of the hardened, unbelieving older people have started their lives as natural worshippers of God, whether or not they were reared by God-fearing people. One may well wonder how this comes about, whether little children are born with illusions which they outgrow later, or whether they have a wisdom at the beginning, which is afterwards lost. Such questions are speculation as long as one assumes that magically, out of nowhere, human souls come into existence at the same moment as their bodies. It is quite another matter if one realises that, when the body is born, the eternal soul passes out of one state of being into another. Before birth, the soul has dwelt among the beings of God in the spheres of the Heavens, from which it must depart when the hour comes to enter the human world on earth. Then one sees the natural awareness of what is divine in little children as the fading remembrance of the other life beyond the gate of birth. They know God, because they have only just left His presence and have not forgotten it, as have those whose childhood is far behind.

The world from which we have come at birth is the same as that into which we shall go at death. But we have forgotten from whence we came, and therefore we look ahead into the unknown as we journey towards the gate of death. In the Divine World our souls have experienced, and will experience again, the oneness of God. Therefore the ungrown child, who is still half in that world, knows the One God. When our souls have entered with their full powers into the world of earth, we can experience the threefoldness of God. Neither is a contradiction of the other, but each is a half of the full cycle of human experience. From above, our souls behold the One God, from below the threefold being of Father, Son and Spirit. Every human being may have both visions in due season, if he is able to pass rightly from childhood into maturity of soul on earth, and out again into the life beyond death.

Every properly grown-up person is capable of apprehending the Trinity, but does not therefore grasp and know the idea. Moreover, this is in need of being discovered again in the present time because, for some while now, it has, under the influence proceeding from the Protestant reformation, been more a theological principle than a living experience. During the age of the Reformation, a great discovery was made, the value and importance of the single human personality. Previously its worth had been felt but little. Since that time the sense of personality has become increasingly precious to each succeeding generation. As individuals grew aware of their own oneness, they consequently directed their attention to the oneness of the Divine World. Prayer became the experience of the single personality addressing the One God. True as this was and still is, one aspect only of the whole relation between God and the human soul can be known after this fashion. It has been the typical Protestant temptation to take the part for the whole. This must inevitably prevent a vision of the Trinity from being found, although the necessary faculties have developed in the mind.

Today the time has come for a new discovery of soul. The image of the threefold Godhead is reflected in the human being. He is one and yet threefold. His self is aware, in the moving life of his soul, of forces of three kinds, those of thinking, feeling and willing. When he knows himself, he sees three spheres interweaving in his nature. In his head he finds the brain and the centre of the nervous system, of which the threads extend throughout his body. Here is concentrated his awareness of thinking. In his heart he feels the pulsing rhythm of his blood and in his breast the in- and out-streaming of the breath. Here he knows the restless surge of his feeling. His limbs are activated with energy that is fed from the centre of the digestive process. Here is the seat of his power of willing, that streams through all parts of the body. So the onefold being, who am I, finds himself actually a trinity.

Simple as such a description is, a great reality lies behind it, which will have far-reaching consequences when they are discovered. The idea of the Trinity, in divine and human form, is most important to the spiritual understanding of modern people. It has been known, in one or another sense, from the beginning of Christianity. Before that time, the idea of the Godhead took two different forms. The Hebrews were chosen to cultivate and develop the conception of the One God. The divine guide who led this people was Jehovah. He was not the ultimate Being who was spoken of by Christ as the Father. He was His representative reflecting the image of the One God whose revelation he made known to the people under his guidance. The other races, who were not Hebrews and who are called in the Bible the Gentiles or the heathens, perceived the manifoldness of God. They were conscious of the Divine World, filled with many beings, whose activity created and nourished the life of people on earth. Behind these manifold and various gods was hidden the divine Unity, apprehended but known in thought only to the most enlightened among men. In those ancient times, people were commonly aware that they shared their existence with a whole multitude of spirits of varied character and powers. They worshipped the great gods, who from time to time appeared on earth to intervene in human affairs. They were familiar with the crowd of less exalted beings, who enlivened the elements of earth, water, air and fire. They were sensitive to the genius of each river and mountain, each ocean and each land. They honoured with sacred rites the spirits who presided in the households, and the members of the family shared with them the domestic hearth. In parts of the globe beyond Europe, this old consciousness of a world filled with a host of beings, who partake in the community of God's universe, still persists today. Those who practise such belief find themselves in contact with demons as much as with benevolent beings. They have to guard themselves against harmful influences and seek the assistance of those that work for good.

Those ancient people, who recognised the oneness of God, and those who beheld His manifoldness, each saw a part of the world-reality. When the turning-point of time was reached and Christ became man, the hour had come of a new birth within evolution. His deed on earth created a reality in the universe that had not existed there before. We know it, from our human standpoint, as the Trinity. By transforming the future destiny of the earthly world, Christ has brought about something new in the history of the Heavens. Before His coming, the Godhead was not yet threefold. In the beginning, at the creation, the Word of God spoke, pouring forth from within that which brought into being the world without. The Word, or Logos, was He whom we call the Son of God. At that time in evolution, the distinction between Father and Son was not yet made. The one was within the other. The Word poured out the divine creating power, in the service of the Divine Will wielding in the whole universe. "The Word was with God." They were united, indivisible, acting out of the unity of all spiritual beings in the Godhead.

Then the created world fell away from the spheres of the Heavens. The presence of God was withdrawn from creation and the princes of Evil unfolded their powers in the forsaken place of existence. Human souls found their destiny in this separated world, where death could penetrate into their nature and evil threaten to destroy them. To rescue the lost race of men, it was resolved in the Divine World to send the Saviour. He came, not to release humans from the fallen world, but to bring them the power of His Spirit to win from death and evil the fruit of freedom. He came to create within Mankind on earth that which could nowhere be harvested in the spheres of the Heavens. He came to transform the place of separation into that of opportunity, to change the weak and helpless human souls into sons of God, in whom death and evil would be overcome. When He descended into the body of Jesus at the baptism in Jordan, He left the Divine World and entered the place from which the real presence of God had been withdrawn. Thereby His own being suffered separation, and He was born out of God into independent existence. Having been with God, He became man on earth. Through that event, He came to know Himself as the Son of the Father-god, who is in the Heavens. In one of the Gospels, two versions are to be found, in the original texts, of the words from Heaven which were to be heard as the dove descended upon Jesus as he was baptised. One of them reads: "Thou art my beloved Son: this day have I begotten thee." In the hour of incarnation the Spirit, who had lived at the beginning in the Logos, was born out of the being of the All-father and entered upon His sonship. That which had been united since before time began was divided for the purpose of bringing salvation to Mankind. When He, who dwells in the Heavens, looked down and beheld departing from Him the One who, until that hour, had been an innate, indivisible part of Himself, He called Him "My Son". When He who went forth from the realms of His true existence looked back to that from whence He came, He said: "Father, who art in the Heavens."

After the baptism in Jordan, Christ Jesus walked with men and women on earth. Throughout this time the Spirit of Christ was penetrating by stages into the bodily vessel offered to Him by Jesus. As the process of incarnation continued, the Son of God entered further into the loneliness of earth-existence. He prayed to the Father and He taught those who followed Him to pray. Only he can pray who recognises that he is separated from the Being to whom his prayer is directed. Where there is no separation, there would be no need of prayer. The words recorded in the Gospels, which the Son spoke while He was on earth to the Father in the Heavens, are the testimony to the relation of the one to the other, which evolved in the course of Christ's life as man. The Son had to become increasingly self-existent. The climax was reached at the crucifixion. In the suffering on the cross, Christ penetrated more deeply than before into the body which He was about to lay aside in death. He reached the most profound experience of Man's separation from his heavenly origins. He sank so far into the depths of loneliness from God that He could repeat the words of the despairing psalm which begins: "My God, why hast thou forsaken me?" This hour of dark experience became illumined by the triumph of Christ's Spirit. His strength was sufficient for the struggle. The light of the Son of God prevailed in the darkness. The glory of the Son's spiritual being shone into the land of shadows as He descended into death. Never before had He had to undertake so much out of the might of His Self-existence. Another interpretation of the words quoted from the psalm reads: "My God, how hast thou glorified Me." To what glory had His sonship flowered! Contradictory as the two interpretations sound, they are actually the shadow-side and the light-side of the same happening.

The Son invaded the realm where death is really present, the place most deeply opposite to the life-filled heights of the Heavens. Following the will of the Father, drinking to the end the cup which He had given (St John, ch. 18), He rose again to earth, uniting His Spirit with this world which had fallen under the dominion of the powers He had vanquished. The earthly world became by His resurrection the kingdom of the Son. At Eastertime He took up His abode there and entered upon His kingship. After the forty days of the Resurrection, those who were with Him saw Him depart, ascending through the doorway of the clouds into Heaven. Though He left their sight, He did not disappear from His kingdom. His Spirit expanded from the earth, without leaving it, to unite again with the universe. The Son returned to the Father, having overcome death and saved from destruction Man, the lost child of God. He restored the world of earth to the heavenly community of the stars, from which it had for so long been alienated. The Sonship which had been initiated, tried and made true on earth was confirmed and made real in the Divine World. The Son was united again with the Father in the Heavens. One part of the Trinity had become a fact in the universe.

Later, at Whitsuntide, the Holy Spirit was given to the apostles. They were assembled, with Mary, in the upper room on the first day of the week when the Spirit descended in a great cosmic thunderstorm. They heard the rushing wind and saw the tongues of lightning strike down upon every head. The Spirit quickened within every heart and living words poured from every mouth. The Comforter, the One who had been promised, who had been sent to help, had come. As the Son-god had been born in the descent from Heaven to earth at the baptism in Jordan, so the Spirit-god came forth from the Father when the tongues of fire entered the hearts of the apostles. The third Person of the Trinity began His separate existence when He came to make His dwelling in the souls of men.

The Holy Spirit had in earlier times worked among men, sending inspiration from the Heavens above, where He dwelt. He was closely related to the Son, overshadowing His being during His life on earth. At Whitsuntide a new evolution began within the course of the divine existence. He became the offering made through the Son by the Father to human souls, for the sake of their salvation. Christ had performed the deed that changed history. The Holy Spirit brought the force of enlightenment, through which the minds of men and women should be enabled to grasp and understand it. Christ had given to human souls the inner power of the true self, by which they should grow, in the course of their evolution, into the likeness of the resurrected Man which He had revealed in Himself. The Holy Spirit came to give clear vision for the Christian ideal and to kindle the flames of enthusiasm in human hearts.

The Holy Spirit is the helper of human souls. At the beginning the children of humanity were created by the Spirit of God. The power of the creation was sufficient to maintain their existence for part of their history, but not until its completion. People were weakened by the sickness of sin and infected with the forces of death. A new power of Spirit, capable of healing their nature from within was bestowed upon them by the grace of the Father and the Son. A new, living impulse has been sent down from the heights of the Heavens, which penetrates into the inmost parts of human souls, overcoming their weakness, healing them from the ills produced by sin and temptation. A wellspring of healing force is hidden within them, poor and weak as they may nevertheless appear on the surface.

At one time the picture for the Holy Spirit was the dove, the pure white bird flying down from the door of Heaven, the messenger of divine inspiration. At Whitsuntide He came in the guise of tongues of flame. Since that event He lives on earth as inner light and warmth in human souls. The future picture of the Holy Spirit will be in human form. He is still in the process of becoming one with the being of Mankind. The Trinity will come to fruition at the end of time, when Man will have attained resurrection. A part of the history of the Son and a still larger part of the history of the Spirit lie in the future, involved with the coming destiny of Man. The Son has passed through birth, death, resurrection and ascension. The Holy Spirit has been little more than born. A great unfolding of His power is still to come. The Trinity as a whole is in the process of evolving towards that which shall be in the future.

For the sake of Mankind, to the end that salvation shall be achieved on earth, the Godhead has become threefold. Father and Son and Holy Spirit have become three in the revelation they have poured out into the world of men. In the life we had before birth, we knew the presence of God, His Oneness filling the Heavens. Here on earth we see His working in ourselves. In the substance of our existence we recognise the Father. In the creating power within us, we feel the Son. In the light shining in our consciousness, we know the Spirit. We behold in the Trinity the gift of God to people on earth. That which exists in us, that which creates in us, that which enlightens us is the Divine that has been made Three in One and One in Three for the sake of our salvation. God offers Himself to human souls as the Father, as the Son and as the Holy Spirit.

ST. JOHN'S TIDE

ST. JOHN'S TIDE

Midsummer is the opposite turning-point in the year to mid-winter, to which the festival of Christmas in linked. The sun has reached the highest point in his progress through the sky and the power of his light, having come to the climax, begins to decrease. Just as the sun starts to turn back to the earth at midwinter, so he turns away at midsummer. This does not affect the experience often to be made, that the weather is hotter after midsummer than before. The Christian festival proper to this season is that of St John. Whereas Christmas is popularly accepted even by unreligious people, St John's tide is overlooked even by a great number of regular churchgoers. Nevertheless it is as much part of the order of the Christian year and should be celebrated in due time. Naturally, since it has long been in disuse, this festival requires particular thought and inquiry into its content and significance.

We follow the course of the summer by the succession of flowers and fruit. It begins with the blossoming of trees and bushes. The flowering time of fruit trees falls mostly within the spring. But we begin to think it is summer when the chestnuts put forth their candle-like flowers, when the laburnums bring out their golden chains and lilac fills the air with scent. The procession of the flowers in the garden beds tell the changing hours of the summer. In the countryside the flowers of woodland, field and hedgerow mark their passing. A distinct change appears at the turn of midsummer. Notice of it is often given by the lime blossom. Its warm sweet scent drifts low on the air, frequently catching us by surprise, when it is encountered some distance from the tree. The essence of summer has been distilled into this aroma welcomed so eagerly by the bees, that their steady warm murmur about the trees is like its counterpart in sound. It is the signal of midsummer and at the same moment another portent becomes visible. The foliage of trees and bushes alters colour, sinking down from the bright green of spring into the dark heavy shade, which quickly, should there be a long spell of dry weather, become tinted with brown. Before this change, each tree has its own colouring from the time when the leaves first emerge from the buds. In the early summer one can look out over a wide landscape and distinguish one tree from another by the shade of the foliage, even at a great distance. After midsummer the colour in the same landscape becomes a uniform dark green, with the slight variation of more silvery hues.

This change is part of another. Flowering gradually gives way to fruiting. The bright petals of the blossoms fade and fall, as their time finishes, to be replaced by the fruits. Hard, green and small at first, they fill out quickly and change colour. The life-forces of a tree or a plant recede from the leaves and flowers, to be concentrated in the seed and fruit. After the turn of the year has passed, the long season of ripening follows. Patches of colour appear in the green countryside. The corn now grown high is turning from green to various shades of yellow, that will later deepen to gold. Trees show the bright colours of their fruit as it reddens in the warmth of the sun. Ripening and harvest begin during the four weeks of St John's tide, which start at midsummer.

At this season the soul of the earth rises in longing towards the heights, seeking communion with the universe, with the light and warmth of the sun and his companions, the stars. At midwinter she has begun to breathe her soul outward to the world above. At midsummer her long outbreathing is completed and her whole soul has gone forth in devotion. At St John's tide a great streaming of life and force surges upwards from the depths.

The plants show it as they thrust to their full height and open their flowers to the sun, breathing out the essence of their being in scent and drifting pollen. The mineral kingdom shows it less openly but as truly. The forces of form impregnating all matter that has crystallised into shape, stream upwards. Matter urges spiritwards in every part of creation. The counterpart has come to the sacred interval of the Holy Nights at Christmas. Then Spirit yearned towards matter raining down the inspiration for the fresh growth of Nature. Now all the earth's creatures yearn towards the Heavens. Matter seeks Spirit, returning to its origin in expansion towards the world-heights.

How is it at this season with Man? What happens to the souls of human beings? They are uplifted in unison with the soul of the earth. We are aware in the summertime of living much more in the world outside than we do in the winter. Yet we live, not down on the earth, but absorbed into the light-filled atmosphere above its surface. Our feet may be as much on the ground as in the winter, but our feelings rise with the sprouting plants and our thoughts expand into the world. The life of our soul yearns upwards. In this season, when the harvest is being prepared, what happens in human existence? Are we only onlookers at the deed of offering to be made by Nature, are we only waiting for the nourishment we hope to receive? Outwardly it might appear so and many people may believe that this appearance is reality. In spiritual fact, it is different. From the hearts of all human beings the moral forces stream out towards the Heavens at this season. When the plants offer up their colour and scent, the minerals their innate power of form, the moving creatures their activity, human souls reveal the moral impulse within their will. The harvest of Humanity that ripened on earth is reaped in the heights, yielding its fruit, both good and bad, to the universe. At no other season does the moral life of Man mingle with the world outside himself as in the time of midsummer.

Mostly without our consciousness, but nevertheless truly, the wickedness and goodness in human thoughts, feelings and deeds is woven into the universe. Failings and errors flow in dark streams of disturbance through the great cloud of offering that rises from creation to the Heavens. The goodness and purity of human hearts mingles in harmony with what is offered to the Spirit of the World in the heights from the kingdoms of the stones, plants and beasts. Mankind must contribute to the surge of devotion streaming from the depths to the heights throughout creation at this season. Good and evil are the fruits of human life that no other creature has to offer. The harvest of the human heart is gathered in the Heavens by the angels. The good is transformed and woven into the light of the universe, finding its fulfilment in the spirit-life of the Divine World. The bad spreads clouds of darkness and disturbance between the earth and the Heavens, revealing its true destructive nature.

The quality in the human heart most roused at this festival is the conscience. It may seem strange that this attribute should belong to midsummer, when our inclination turns naturally to holidays out of doors and relaxation. It is so pleasant to slip into a carefree dream, while Nature sinks into the summer sleep that comes upon her when the soul of the earth aspires heavenward. But whenever human beings become wholly absorbed in the moods of Nature they are in danger. We should not allow ourselves to fall into a sleep of the mind but we should seek in the natural relaxation of summertime a new acquaintance with the force of conscience. This is a quality which should in the present age come into a further stage of development. Our consciences are sensitive to our personal faults, to blemishes in behaviour, to lapses from the pattern of what we would wish to be before ourselves and before others. The conscience of which we should become aware in St John's tide is less personal and more universal. When each one realises that he is individually a part of Mankind, a member of the race, responsible for the earth, one of the order of beings, which form a hierarchy below that of the angels, he finds another kind of conscience. The history of man becomes his concern. The human part in the order of the universe is of interest to him. The cosmic nature of the earth in community with the stars of Heaven becomes real to his imagination. The capacity we need to enliven this conscience of universal proportions is that of using imagination in a cosmic sense. The summer season is proper for this purpose. We live then less closely in our personal selves, less tightly wrapped up in our own affairs. The mind can expand more freely into the world and feel more vividly the life of the universe.

In the centre of the Christian festival at this season stands the figure of John the Baptist. Its name is his name. In the whole cycle of the Christian festivals only this one is under the sign of a human figure. It is essentially the festival of Man. At Whitsuntide the Holy Spirit descended to Mankind and from this gift of the Father in the Heavens proceeds the festival of Man to follow it. Perhaps one of the reasons why this portion of the Christian year is so overlooked comes from the unwillingness of people to realise their humanity. The figure of John, guardian of this festival, is awe-inspiring. Is this the dignity of Man to which we aspire? The picture of John is disquieting now, as it was in the time of his earthly life to the people of his generation. To expect little of oneself as a human being is more comfortable, calling for less effort of conscience, than to face what is expressed in the being of John. The word "humanity" has two distinct uses. It may be an expression for the greatest weakness and frailty, in the sense of saying "to err is human". It may be the word for the highest calling and dignity of Man. That may be summed up within it which is intended by the old words from the mysteries: "Man, become what thou art." The festival of St John makes us aware that we must decide between the two if we would celebrate it rightly. We cannot but accept the latter sense and reverence the highest ideal in the word "humanity".

Just as we experience at this season the more than personal nature of our conscience, so we can in this festival lift up our thoughts about the being of Man into the sphere of cosmic conceptions. Man is a creature of the universe, with a place in its order, having fellowship with all other beings who live and move therein. The idea of Man, which is borne in the mind of God is the hidden treasure in each one of us children of the human race. When we contemplate the figure of St John, we are beholding a picture of that which we can find in ourselves, when we think to look for it. Moreover, we realise through this picture what the beings of God, the angels, archangels and all the company of Heaven look for when their gaze turns earthward to the life of men and women. Much that makes up our personal life is in their eyes only husk and rind within which is wrapped the living soul, the tiny germ that has still to grow and mature. What we human inhabitants of the earth are at present is unsatisfactory, unfulfilled from the angelic point of view. Their interest is directed to what we can and should become in the course of time. We understand and recognise their picture of Man, we share their outlook, when we contemplate what the figure of St John represents in the festival of midsummer.

John the Baptist was the herald of Christ's coming. He performed the deed of baptism through which His Spirit could enter the soul and the body prepared by Jesus for His sake. From the cosmic heights of Heaven into the depths of earth He descended who was the Son of God becoming Man. He, who bore within Himself the Spirit-light of the universe, left His dwelling at the heart of the world in the sun, to carry the power of love down into the life of Mankind. Although few of those whom He came to help, recognised and accepted Him, one waited for His coming with a heart filled with devotion and lit by enthusiasm. John spoke of himself as the friend of the bridegroom, who rejoiced to hear His voice. He became the first in the company of human souls who wish to acknowledge Christ and follow Him. He was called to perform the first act by which a human being could share in the task undertaken by the Son of God on earth when he baptised Jesus. The Heavens opened and God the Father spoke in the heights. In that hour the veil between earth and Heaven was parted and the work of God was done by the hands of a man. The Father, the Son and the man John were joined in a Trinity by the act through which Christ descended into human form.

St John's tide is the festival when the eyes of our human minds should be lifted up to see the Heavens opened and to recognise how God and Man are related to each other in the universe. The season of Midsummer naturally draws our interest outside ourselves to the drama of blossoming and fruiting in Nature. Our souls breathe deeply in the light-filled spaces of the air and enjoy the warmth of the world. In the festival of St John we find the spiritual counterpart to this natural experience. We lift up our hearts to feel the cosmic existence of God and to realise therewith the universal being of Man. The human figure of John is the sign of the festival, which reminds us that the Christian destiny of Man is to become the Son of God.

JOHN

The name John is used in the Bible, not in the personal sense it has today, but to designate a part of that which belongs to all human beings. In the Greek it is composed of three vowels, i, o and a, finishing with the consonants n and s. Among people of ancient times, who listened much more than we today to the life within the single sound, these vowels were understood to express the pure substance of the soul, born out of the power of God, enclosed in earthly shape by the consonants. John was the title for one whose inner being revealed the divine qualities that live in a true man. Everyone has, in a sense, a "Ioanes" within him, but its original purity has rarely been preserved.

In the Gospels two men are called John. One is the Baptist, who prepared the way for the Messiah. The other is the apostle, who was likewise the evangelist, the author of epistles, and the seer of the Apocalypse. Some readers have been unable to imagine personality in all these capacities and have argued that more than one person stands behind these writings. Others believe that there was but one. These two men were the first to begin bringing to revelation within them the true Christian nature. They both richly inherited the fruits of humanity that had matured in Mankind through the course of its long history, and brought the wealth of the past as an offering to Him, who had come to take human destiny upon Himself. They became the first in whom the pattern of new Christian manhood could be brought to light. That the new humanity might be born in them, the old had to die. Neither could become thoroughly penetrated with the Christian impulse until he had passed through the experience of death.

John the Baptist fulfilled in his character and destiny all that the Jews of his day expected of a man chosen for the service of God. The circumstances of his birth were such as to cause wonder and mark him out as a child of promise. His father was a priest in the temple with a reputation for piety that was shared by his mother. These good-living people remained childless until they were so advanced in age as to lose hope of children. The father was carrying out his duties in the temple one day, when the angel Gabriel appeared to him and promised him a son who was to be called John. The meeting with the angel caused him to lose his power of speech until the day of the child's birth. When the elderly mother Elizabeth was waiting for the child to be born, she was visited by Mary, the young maiden to whom the angel Gabriel had foretold that she would be the mother of Jesus. The two unborn children greeted each other while they were still in the womb, and the mothers were together for three months. The boy Jesus was born at midwinter, and John came into the world half a year earlier at midsummer. He was given the name chosen by the angel, and the father recovered his power of speech.

This child of promise grew up and early turned his back on worldly affairs and interests. He chose to retire into the desert and become a hermit. He was very sensitive to the tense mood of expectation among the Jews at that time. The Messiah must soon appear. John concentrated all the forces of his being upon listening for the voice of God, upon preparing for the world-event that must be at hand. He made himself homeless, living on the simplest food and wearing the roughest clothing. He was conforming to the pattern by which prophets were made, according to the standard accepted by the people around him. He was eagerly sought out and begged to proclaim a message from Heaven. His stern words and upright counsel were greatly respected. It is easy to imagine how much more readily he was understood by those around him than the Messiah when He actually appeared. John was everything that people could hope and many were willing to take him for the Messiah. Jesus Christ, on the other hand, behaved in many ways quite differently from that which was expected of the long-awaited God. There is little doubt that John was, for a long while, the more famous of the two and attracted a greater following.

John knew that he had a mission from God to become the herald who would prepare the way for the One who was to come. He was to be the voice proclaiming the message of the Lord, after the manner of the old prophets. The keynote to what he preached was the cry translated in the English of the Authorised Version by the word "repent". It would be more accurately rendered into modern language by such a phrase as: change your hearts and minds. He said to his hearers: to prepare for the great event to come, you must thoroughly change the direction of your thoughts and feelings. You must put off the old human nature and make yourselves ready to be born again. When the listening people asked him to interpret his counsel in their daily affairs, he gave practical advice. He told the soldiers, the tax-gatherers and others how to have a conscience in their dealings with their fellows. He did not, as many other Jewish teachers would have done, teach the observance of the Law of Moses. He preached about the individual sense for right and wrong, which could be exercised by those, like the Roman soldiers, who were not children of Abraham, as much as by those who were of the chosen race. A change of heart had to come about in his hearers before they could even listen to such sayings, so revolutionary at that time were conceptions of this kind. John's outer appearance and way of life were orthodox, but what he preached went far beyond the old tradition. The Jews around him put all their faith in being members of a chosen people, founded by Abraham. John proclaimed that the tree of their race was old and ripe for the axe. They should be prepared to be born again out of that which was to come.

John performed the rite of baptism by water for his followers. What they heard when he preached became deep, living experience, penetrating into the depths of their inner nature, when they were baptised. In those days the ceremony of being dipped under water for the sake of spiritual purification was not in the least symbolic, as it needs must be today. Those who were baptised were actually brought by shock to the verge of death and came back to life with the experience of being born again. While this happened to the disciples of John, they beheld a vast picture of past history, not that of themselves but of the human race. They saw in a vision how Mankind had proceeded at the beginning from God, how, through the lures of Evil, human beings had fallen into the state of separation from the Divine World, how they were in danger of being destroyed by sin and death. They knew, from intense individual experience, that Mankind could no longer survive unless a divine Saviour would come to help, that the hour of crisis and change was at hand. The bodies of people were at that time so different from ours today that they were able to survive coming into close touch with death, which would now be impossible. For the remainder of their lives they carried in their hearts the knowledge that had been gained through their baptism.

The sacred rite, by which the Baptist purified his hearers from spiritual blindness and fear of leaving what was past, was made into the means by which Jesus of Nazareth could give up his soul and body to the Spirit of Christ. Jesus came to John and was baptised by him in the River Jordan. The eternal soul of Jesus withdrew and the being of Christ entered the human form which had been prepared for Him. John, representing in that hour the whole of Mankind, performed the human act which was necessary that the

Son of God might fulfil His resolve to become the Son of Man. He who knew himself to be the herald was called to become the birth-helper of the Messiah. He recognised with full heart what had taken place, who had come. "He must increase, but I must decrease. He who cometh from above is above all" (St John, ch. 3, v. 30). What he preached, what he effected through his baptism, was always to his mind the preparation for that which would be much greater. He pointed not to himself but to the Other, who, coming after, was yet preferred before him. That which was most characteristic of him was pictured by the artist who painted him as an upright figure in the act of pointing with a forefinger, out of all proportion larger than his other limbs, to Jesus Christ.

After the greatest of his baptisms, John continued to work with his followers as before. He did not become one of the disciples of Jesus. The evangelists Matthew and Luke tell how, some time later, he sent some of his own pupils to Jesus to ask: "Art thou He that should come, or look we for another?" (St Luke, ch. 7, v. 20; St Matthew, ch. 11, v. 3). Should we imagine that later on John was himself not certain that the Messiah was come? He was the last of the old race of Hebrew prophets, who spoke and acted when inspired, not out of their own minds but as messengers of the Lord. He did not doubt his mission nor his message. He knew that at the baptism of Jesus he had acted as the Spirit of God directed. His later uncertainty of mind came from another part of his being, from the human part, which fell short in understanding of that which spoke through him under inspiration. The prophet outdistanced the man in him, not at all times but at moments. Such was the inevitable shadow cast by the pre-Christian manner of inspiration over the souls of those who were called to be the messengers of the Lord.

After a while John fell a victim to the tyrant Herod and, at the request of Salome, the daughter of Herodias, was beheaded.

He forfeited his life to the adversary. Was his death a sacrifice to protect Him whom he had baptised? Nothing is said on this point in the Gospels. John's mission had been fulfilled in the sense that He for whom he prepared the way had come. The last of the prophets had finished his task and could lay down his life. Nevertheless, the story of his end, so soon after the coming of Christ, is reminiscent of the fate of the children of Bethlehem, who were massacred when Jesus was born. The powers that wished to hinder the birth of the Messiah were actively present on both occasions, and perhaps a sacrifice to them was, in fact, necessary. At all events, it is very likely that Herodias, who planned the murder, wished that Herod himself should appear to the Jews as the god who had become man. She may well have feared that John would prevent this scheme or be acclaimed as Messiah himself.

An old legend tells that the companions of Jesus in his childhood were the souls of the children massacred in Bethlehem. The Gospels point, by their manner of describing the death of John, to a new relation to Christ, which his soul formed after he was released from the body. In life he had kept distant from Jesus and the apostles. In death he came into a close companionship with them. The first sending out of the disciples by Christ, to preach and to heal in His absence, is brought together in the Gospels with the beheading of John. The circle of the Twelve became mature and established as a community at that time. Christ could begin to pour His virtue of healing into the group of apostles, and His Spirit began to work through them, even when He was not actually present. The Twelve had been called by Christ to be His first community. Time and growth were necessary before they could begin to become that which they were intended to be. Another element was needed in addition, which was provided after the death of John.

When a group of individuals becomes a community, a guardian spirit has to attach himself to the whole circle before their common being can be made real and true. Such a process is to be observed in community-forming of every kind. From whence would the guardian being of the Twelve be found? After his death, the spirit of John the Baptist was able to draw near to Christ and to relate himself in this manner to the apostles. He overshadowed them, guarded their ways and held them together in a community, that was being prepared and trained to serve the Spirit of Christ. John, who had not been a disciple, united himself in spirit with the twelve apostles, after he had lost his life on earth. His death was transformed into a baptism through which he entered upon a new existence devoted to helping the followers of Christ to fulfil their task. From the spirit-heights to which his soul was lifted when he passed out of the body, he could behold what was still obscure to those who were still walking in this world. He was able to watch Christ's life, His passion, death and resurrection, with spiritual insight. He, more clearly than they who were still confined to the body, saw that a deed of God was performed on earth.

John the Baptist showed in his being and character the grace of soul and spirit that flowered within human nature before the coming of Christ. He was therefore able to walk with God after the manner of those who received divine inspirations in the ancient fashion which came in him to its end. The other John of the Gospels was the first among men to show in his being the Christian forces and to receive inspiration by the new way which was initiated at that time. As the Baptist was the last of the prophets, so was John the first of the apostles. He was not able to become the earliest Christian soul without undergoing an experience of death and second birth through the power of Christ. Before this great transformation his name was not yet John. In the fourth Gospel he is called Lazarus, the brother of Martha and Mary. Another tradition says that he was also the rich young man who came to Jesus and was filled with sorrow to hear that he must part with his riches (St Luke, ch. 18, v. 18). Lazarus will have been a man who inherited much of the spiritual wealth from the great cultures of the previous ages. It is not difficult to imagine that he found it hard to understand that he must first release himself from this before he could truly receive the Christian impulse into his being. The wealth of the past would then be lost for a while, to rise again in a Christian form at a later time in history. The young man may well have passed through a great inner struggle before he could accept this and, with the two sisters, become the devoted follower of Jesus Christ.

The name of John became his after Lazarus had passed through his initiation and been called from the tomb to new life by Christ (St John, ch. 11). He is not, in fact, called by this name in St John's Gospel. There he has a title in place of a name, which is used for him when he was still Lazarus (ch. 11, v. 3) and when he was the disciple sitting closest to the Master at the Last Supper (ch. 13, v. 23). It is found again in the story of the Resurrection, when some of the disciples met the Risen One by the lake at dawn (ch. 21, v. 7). This title is: "the one whom Jesus loved". The other evangelists gave this apostle the name "John", but he in his own Gospel spoke of himself by the title without a name. In modern language, this phrase may sound as if it meant that he was the best-loved friend of the Master among the disciples. In the old speech of the Gospels it has no such flavour of personal preference. It is a term often used in the language of the old mystery-temples, where initiations were performed, to describe the relation between the high priest and the one who has passed through the sacred rite of death and rebirth at his hands. Spiritual love of a kind unlike ordinary affection united the souls of the two who stood in such a relation to one another. The death of Lazarus was part of the initiation performed on him by Christ Himself, who acted as the high priest. After that time the old form of initiation was no longer necessary.

A new process, which takes place inwardly, has in the Christian era replaced the old. When Lazarus came back to life, he had so far become a new person that he was later known by the sacred name of John. The Baptist had the name because he was "the man sent from God" (St John, ch. 1, v. 6). He represented the divine in Man which had been given at the creation, in the beginning. The apostle became John because he was the man sent from Christ. He had in the process of initiation received into his being the divine power, the indwelling Spirit, given to the human soul by Him who had come to save Mankind from destruction.

John the apostle was he who had once been Lazarus. Yet in the Gospels, long before the story of his rising from the dead, the name is found in the list of the Twelve beside that of James and both are called the sons of Zebedee. The circle of the apostles, who walked on earth with Jesus Christ and who founded, after receiving the gift of the Holy Spirit, the Christian Church, was not in the first place a group of personalities. It was a community representing in twelve parts the whole of Mankind. Each man represented much more than himself. The apostles were capable of becoming the chosen messengers of their Master, because they were able to carry in their being more than their own personalities. A picture from another part of history illumines the nature of this inner circle of disciples. At a later time, the British king Arthur spread the influence of Christianity through his wild land with the assistance of the twelve chosen knights of the Round Table. At certain times the knights gathered at the king's court and the table was prepared for the festival. There were twelve seats, inscribed with twelve names, and once it happened that no one was found to take the twelfth place until a strange youth appeared. He proved himself able to occupy the seat and bear the name. As at the Round Table, so in the circle of the apostles, there were twelve places, having names attached to them, and twelve kinds of human beings throughout the race of men, who belonged to them. The disciples who gathered round Jesus Christ were the first who became members of the original community of Christians, the circle of the Twelve. In truth, each human soul has a place there and in his inner being has a relation to one or the twelve names. No one is excluded from striving to become an apostle, who seeks to make alive in himself the forces of Christ. The circle is twelve-fold, but every human being may approach one of the twelve places, if he can bear the name that is written there.

More than one personality could be present among the apostles in the place which belonged to the name of John. The son of Zebedee and he who had been Lazarus were, in fact, distinct persons, of whom at times the one was present in the circle and at times the other, during the events described in the Gospels. Lazarus-John was he who became, in the Acts of the Apostles, the companion of Peter and, later still, the evangelist, the author of St John's epistles, and the seer of the Apocalypse. In these writings, each one of the three entirely different from the others, the inner character appears, which ripened within him as the fruit of his initiation into the new mystery of Christianity. In that experience his inner being had been penetrated by the influence of Christ. The forces of his soul, thinking, feeling and willing, were directed towards comprehending and realising what he had beheld.

In his epistles, he wrote to his followers that which had ripened from long pondering in his heart. His devotion and reverence to the living mystery, which he had known and witnessed from the beginning, were poured out for those to receive, whose hearts he wished to enkindle and rejoice. In his Gospel the strength of his transformed thinking is revealed. All four Gospels were composed out of spiritual revelation, but the evangelists each received that for which they had developed the necessary insight. None of the four is inspired by such strong forces of thought as that of John. The other three contain many parables, or spiritual truth in likenesses, but the fourth describes the ideas in word-pictures which come straight from the thinking of Christ. John was able to see straight into the thoughts of his Master, while the other evangelists more often caught their reflection. In the Revelation of St John we read that which came to him through his enlightened will. He looked into the secrets of coming evolution, as it will appear through the active presence of Christ in the history of the world. The purpose of Him who has taken the destiny of Mankind upon Himself appeared to John as if they would be his own. His willing was united with the word-willing of Him whom he followed.

The apostle John became the first Christianised human being, in that his feeling, thinking and willing became filled with Christian forces. Christianity became a living power on earth through his being, as it will do through that of everyone who becomes truly Christian. In this he fulfilled that which was begun by John the Baptist. After his death, the Baptist could accompany and watch with insight the deed of Christ. He could shelter and inspire the community of the Twelve. But, being outside the body, he could not transform what he beheld into will. Another, who had returned from death back to bodily existence, had to found Christianity in the reality of earthly life. The one John was the herald of Christ, the other His first apostle. Both bore the same name, for what was prophesied in the one was fulfilled in the other. They were the pioneers in the great process that will continue, in the future, to the end of evolution, the making Christian of human souls.

BETWEEN ST. JOHN'S TIDE
AND MICHAELMAS

THE SUN ON EARTH

Summer is the time when the earth opens up her secrets. She displays her treasures slowly, letting the buds swell and mature gently until the flower is due to emerge from the sheath and expand into full-blown glory. One after another the trees and plants attain the culminating moment of flowering, each held in check until its due season has arrived. Summer has so much to bring forth in a short space that she can fill the whole season with a succession of beauties. The delight of this time is to watch the secrets, which she kept hidden away in the dark and cold of winter, unfold one by one in the warmth of the sun's light. She is spreading wide her mysteries before the face of the sun. In the midst of winter she had listened to what he could tell her of the wisdom treasured among the stars. In summer she reaches up towards the Heavens, bringing to light, after her own manner, what she has known within herself.

The sun is turned towards the earth in summertime, drawing with his warm, bright beams her soul up towards the heights. In his rays and in the falling streams of the rain the gifts of the Heavens are sent down to earth and to all her living creatures. When the flowers fade, the seeds, formed at the centre of the blossoms, ripen in the husks, which gradually wither and, as they split open, release their wealth. The heaven-sent warmth of the sunbeams quickens the dark, small seeds with the forces of light and life. The sun's gift of one summer will be preserved in the ground through the winter until the next. When the strengthening rays begin again in the following spring to draw up the shoots and touch open the buds, the sun's treasure of the previous summer is put forth in blossom. He gives to the earth the interchange of seasons. He is the life-giver and then the witherer. Through him the plants are burnt up. Flowering is followed by decay. The watery life of the plant is sucked up in the heat of his beams. But, as the leaves droop and the flowers wither, the seed is impregnated with the life of the universe. Under the dominion of the sun the earth passes through the round of the year, continuing the evolution of her existence.

To outward view, the sun and the earth follow their yearly movement, drawing together in summer, moving apart in winter. Something, however, has changed in the sphere of spiritual realities. Christ is the Lord of the sun, and when He came down to earth He left His dwelling empty of His presence. The outer sun can still maintain his function in the sky. The true heart of the sun is not there but in the world of earth. When Jesus Christ walked among men, the Sun-spirit was within Him. When Christ rose again after the death on the cross, the Sun-spirit was born into the soul of the earth herself. The sun looks down and beholds his Spirit dwelling on earth.

When the disciples walked with Jesus Christ they became the beams shining from the sun. So it was when the five thousand were fed. The sixth chapter of St John's Gospel tells how the disciples accompanied Him over the Sea of Galilee and to the top of a mountain. A great crowd of people followed them, gathering on the slopes of the hillside. Christ sat on the summit, with the twelve close about Him and the mass of people forming a wider circle round them. The other evangelists tell how evening fell upon this scene. St John leaves this to be assumed from the event happening in the night, which follows in the same chapter. Yet he adds a curious, significant detail: "now there was much grass in the place". The description sounds like that of a lush meadow, where the feet would sink deep among the thick tufts. But the place is the topmost slope of a mountain, or at least of a high hill. Such difficulties of interpretation in the Gospels are often explained away by a small amount of ingenuity. A number of ways could be found to get round one of this kind. Another alternative arises if one decides to read the words of the Gospels in a different manner. One can observe such a discrepancy and see it as a riddle. If one inquires further into the nature of the riddle, it shows itself to be the sign of a secret hidden behind the outer description of the scene. In a certain sense, the Gospels are written in code, that is to say with a deeper level of meaning below the surface. It is not hidden, but it is indicated in a peculiar way, which requires reading between the lines to understand. A discrepancy, unless it is due to faulty translation of the original, is most often the sign that a deeper meaning is to be found at this point.

Nothing is more improbable than that the top of a mountain by the Sea of Galilee would have been outwardly and physically a grassy meadow. Quite a different aspect is seen if these words are so read as to say that the people experienced themselves sitting on plentiful green grass. Such an experience can happen to a person as he is falling asleep. The outer appearance of the world fades away from his notice, and his soul begins to pass over into the sphere of the life-forces, into the living mantle which envelops the earth. Should he not yet be quite overcome by sleep, he would see this sphere in a dream-picture representing growth and renewal. Sinking down upon a meadow of grass would be the most likely form for such an experience to take. That is to say, these few words in verse 10 can be read to say that night was coming on, when a great crowd of human souls, passing out of the body as they fell asleep, converged upon Christ and His disciples in their seclusion. The wording may mean that the people actually followed them across the lake and slept near to them on the mountain. It is equally open to imagine that they had not physically left their homes, but that as they slept their great longing to be with Christ carried their souls into His presence. He perceived them gathering round Him by spiritual sight and such was His power that the disciples could behold with Him the great crowd of hungering souls.

This whole event took place in the spheres of sleep, when the souls were out of their bodies. The spiritual strength of Christ gave to the apostles the grace to be awake while they were outwardly asleep and dreaming. They went into this experience without being able to grasp it. Their Master wished to rouse them to realisation. He asked Philip a question, of such a kind that he might have awakened thereby to the fact that they were foregathered in a realm where physical laws no longer held good. His answer showed that he was still unaware. Nevertheless, Jesus Christ began the sacred act of feeding the hungry souls in sleep, and the apostles were allowed to be His helpers. He accepted the offering that the souls brought to Him, that is to say, He took from the young lad the five loaves and the two fishes. Who is the lad? He is the living picture of the natural, unspoilt innocence that is enshrined in almost every human heart, however hardened and tarnished the exterior that covers it. The child in the human soul, the inheritance of our origin in the world of God, is made visible in this scene in the young lad who had something to offer Christ, some fruit of earth-existence carried over from waking to sleeping. He could accept the pure and innocent offering. Giving thanks, He divided it among the disciples to carry to the people.

The small offering became food for the whole multitude of people, and fragments were left to be gathered up at the close of the meal. Spiritual nourishment, pictured as bread and fish, was given to the starving souls of men. Falling asleep is always a seeking for refreshment. The forces of the body are renewed while the soul is absent in the world of Spirit looking to be refreshed with goodness and wisdom. In sleep the inner being of Man should drink of the spiritual influences of the stars and be fed with the moral truth of the Heavens. When Christ came to earth, the world below and the Divine World above had become so divided, so shut off from one another by a great gulf, that the souls of men and women were no longer nourished spiritually from above, not even in the time that was passed in sleep. He came to bring again the gifts of Heaven to earth, to renew with spiritual grace the sick and hungry being of Man. He gathered the small harvest of innocent goodness that still grew in human hearts and multiplied it with the forces He fetched down from the stars in the Heavens. So He fed the sleeping souls and restored to them the living virtues from which they could, in waking life, begin to grow in the grace of true humanity.

The feeding of the five thousand took place while Christ was on earth, but it was not quite of an earthly character. Later, by His death on the cross, He gave the spiritual food of His body and blood for the earth's renewal in an act of offering that was as true in the physical sphere as in the spiritual. After His resurrection His apostles learnt from Him to celebrate the Christian Sacrament of offering, consecration and communion. The first step on their way to priesthood had been the experience of the night when they received from His hands the consecrated bread and fish to give as a communion to the multitude of sleeping souls. What had begun then in the sphere of sleep was born after the deed of Golgotha into the waking life of day, and was transformed into the Sacrament ordained by Christ, in which bread and wine become spiritual food for soul and body.

The apostles were given the heavenly food to carry to the crowd of waiting people. They were called to be ministers in the Sacrament celebrated by Christ for the sake of human souls. Their priesthood began in this act which, though it was veiled in sleep, was none the less spiritually real and true. What was then begun in secret became an open, earthly fact in Christ's offering of Himself on the cross. His own being was consecrated and transformed by the process in which, out of the death of His earthly nature, He rose again to live with Mankind in the spiritual form of the resurrection. When this was accomplished, the priesthood that had been prepared in the apostles could be completed and fulfilled. They became celebrants of the Christian sacraments, continuing on the altars that which Christ Himself initiated in the act of resurrection.

The apostles were called to be the beams of Christ's sun, carrying into this darkened world the light and life of the Spirit. Every Christian soul since then shares in the apostleship, in the sense of becoming a Christ-bearer. Human beings cannot exist only from that which the outer sun gives to the earth and which she radiates back again to him. Their spirits live from the light of the Spirit-sun who shines, not downwards from above, but outwards from within. Words spoken by human lips, deeds done by human hands, can in the celebration of a living Christian Sacrament be the instrument by which the Spiritual Sun rises for human souls. Each one may kindle the flame in his own heart at this shining fire, of which the radiance is love. The Spirit of Christ is with us, The Sun is on earth.

THE WIDOW'S SON OF NAIN

When autumn comes, death moves swiftly through the kingdom of Nature, turning at a touch the living green of foliage to the yellows, reds and browns that flare up on the fire which consumes the summer. Nature sinks down in this fire and dies once more at the approach of winter. Her beauty is consumed in the fire of decay and passes away until the next season of unfolding.

In ancient times before the incarnation of Christ, a sacred drama which foreshadowed His coming was enacted in the autumn by those peoples who worshipped the god Adonis. He, the god, appeared in the drama as a beautiful youth who died, was mourned by his followers, and, after three days of grief, was beheld by them rising up out of the tomb. The drama ended in rejoicing over his new birth. By means of this sacred festival, the souls of the worshippers were directed to the experience that, when Nature dies in the fire of the autumn, a power of life rises up within human beings while she declines in the world without. In those days, when people lived more intensely in Nature than they can do today, the worshippers learnt each year that the Spirit within the being of Man has vitality and strength of itself although death darkens the world outside.

When Christ walked on earth, the Son of God appeared among men. When He spoke and acted, there was none of the meaninglessness in His words and deeds that so often makes empty those of men and women. What He said and did was filled with spiritual significance, like the words and deeds of a mystery-play, enacted in life. The scenes from the Gospels are reminiscent of the sacred dramas which were part of religious worship in ancient times. They are in no sense their imitations. They repeat in reality what had been performed in the temples in symbol. Although similar characters appear in the scenes, the drama was changed when Christ acted. It was brought on to the stage of history and fulfilled through His presence. One of these scenes related to the old mysteries is the raising of the widow's son at Nain. The young man, dead in the flower of his youth, is carried by mourning companions and attended by his mother, who is a widow. Christ meets the procession and, entering into the drama, He transforms it with the words: "Young man, I say unto thee arise."

Each year in the autumn we come to the experience which is expressed in this picture. If Christ had not renewed our existence on earth by his deed on Golgotha, we should not be able to find the life of the Spirit rising within, when the life of the world outside dies away. At Eastertime on the cross He performed the cosmic deed of death and resurrection. Towards Michaelmas, that which was done for the universe is echoed within each human soul who seeks to be aware of the Spirit. Nevertheless, the fact recorded by St Luke as the raising of the widow's son has a still wider interpretation than that which belongs to the course of the year. This deed brought to life for all time a new form of communion between human souls and the Divine Spirit. What happens again and again in the autumn re-echoes the transformation that was brought about in a single event taking place once at the turn of history.

The young man dwelt in the city of Nain, the name of which means "pasture". It lies not far from the holy mountain Tabor. He lived at a definite date in a place to be found on the map. The inner meaning shines through these outer facts of destiny. The young man was alive at the same time as Jesus Christ and the true purpose of his life was to meet Him at the necessary moment. He lived in a place that provided the most fitting scenery for the event. In the background stood the sacred mountain, the reminder of the Divine World, that looks down upon the plain of earth. Around Nain itself was the pasture, the sign of growth and new life. The youth of the widow's son was reflected in the Nature around him. At a given moment he died, because he could not grow beyond youth to maturity. His strength was finished, and he had to turn back on the road of earthly life. He was dead and being carried to burial when Christ met him.

The disciples came up the hill with their Master as the funeral procession came down, or so it would appear. Christ had compassion on the widowed mother. Whence came this compassion? Did He pity those who had to die, and rescue one such by calling him back to earth? Can it be imagined that He who knew the whole riddle of human existence could wish to prevent a soul from returning to the world of the Heavens, out of which he had come forth when he passed through the gate of birth? The words of the Gospel say that His compassion was for the mother. She, like the son, was an actual person, who lived in a certain time and place. Yet both were more than ordinary beings. They were souls of such stature that they could take part in the cosmic deed enacted by Christ on earth. They represented something in the history of all mankind. They were figures in a mystery-play that was performed in the sphere of fact.

The idea of the widow was a well-known religious conception at that time. The Egyptians knew a divine widow, the goddess Isis, seeking the body of the murdered Osiris. The widow of Nain was not just a woman, weeping for her personal grief alone. Her loss and her pain reflected the fate of all Humanity. Isis was the soul of the Universe, who had lost her divine partner, the mysterious Osiris, who appeared sometimes as husband, sometimes as son. The widow of Nain stood for the soul of Mankind. She was widowed of the Divine Spirit and bereaved of her son, Man, who could not survive youth and become mature in his earthly destiny.

The compassion of Christ was for the whole of Mankind, whose earth-existence had become empty and full of grief. The failure of human destiny is expressed in the picture of the widowed mother and the dead son. "Young man, I say unto thee, arise" were words spoken to Man. The new-born power of the Spirit to awaken and quicken his dying nature streams through them. The mother received the son. The soul received anew the Spirit, by virtue of which she could live in the power to become and to fulfil.

The young man was not restored unchanged to the mother. He had been unable to outlive his youth. The secret of this fact lies in the development that is accomplished in a human being who grows up to manhood. In childhood and youth he lives from the forces that are given him from outside himself. He has come through the gate of birth, and for a while, it remains partly open. The divine beings who nourish our human life can work from their starry dwellings above into the nature of the growing child. Then gradually the working of these forces weakens. The world around him gives him the power to mature. Parents and teachers care for his development. In youth there comes to flower in him all the riches he has received from above, from around, and from below. But when youth is left behind he must begin to live from within. He has to conjure out of himself the forces with which to make his life. He has to become capable of giving where he previously received. At the time when Christ came to earth, mankind could no longer live only from that which the beings of the Divine World had given him in the process of creation. Before that moment the life of Man on earth had been a childhood and youth, nourished continually by divine gifts from outside himself. The danger had come that Man would not survive the youth of his earth-existence, that his being would die away before his destiny was accomplished. Christ called the young man to arise by the power of the Spirit from within. His words were life. He gave through His divine nature the new impulse to the second part of Man's destiny on earth. He gave the power, which continues to work in us, to live from what is brought forth from within, to transform the divine treasure implanted in Humanity into the capacity to give creatively of ourselves.

Within each individual lifetime the crisis comes, which is described in St Luke's Gospel in the story of Nain. In our present age of history it is most likely to occur at about the age of twenty-eight. Until that time we live largely by the grace of the Divine World, of the people around us and of the world into which we have been born. These forces die away slowly and leave the soul in a void. The remaining space of life is to be lived from within, out of the creative spirit hidden in the soul, out of the will to give because one has received. If this crisis is never resolved, if the inner decision is never made in the years that follow, the whole being is lamed. Nevertheless, Christ is our companion on the way through life. Through Him we receive the new impulse, if we will accept it.

The decision to live from the Spirit within, after youth has passed, is not made once for all. It has to become the Christian attitude to life, which is renewed again and again. Today this is true, not only for each single human being, but for Mankind who as a whole faces this decision. The power which was first given to Man, when the widow's son was raised, matures in the present time and all Humanity should attain manhood. The divine beings now pass over the making of history into the sphere of human responsibility. What Man has received by grace has become his inner treasure. Now the Divine World waits for what shall come forth when he who has received gives. Man stands before the void, but he is not alone in his earthly destiny. Christ is present, reminding him of the widow's son, speaking continually to the human heart His word: "I say unto thee, arise."

MICHAELMAS

MICHAELMAS

At the end of September, just after the autumn solstice when the days and nights are of equal length, comes the festival of Michaelmas. The name is still preserved in diaries and calendars but very little is associated with it today. Like the festival of St John it is often overlooked because its significance has become vague and uncertain. Such festivals can acquire new meaning in the present and for the future. They have less tradition than those that fall in the winter and in the spring seasons but they are just as significant in the round of the whole year.

Michaelmas comes in the autumn. The last flowers are in blossom, the leaves are losing their summer green and turning brown and yellow. The fruit has ripened and the harvest has been almost gathered in from the fields. Seeds of every kind are dropping from pods and husks into the ground, ready for the next season. The season of the present year has faded away, giving its force to the germ of life for the season to come. The sun is sinking lower in the Heavens and the warmth of his beams is weakening with the shortening days. The soul of the earth is drawing inwards, turning in upon herself away from the cosmic heights. She begins to awaken out of the dream of summer into the thoughtfulness of winter.

During the summer months the souls of men and women have been drawn upwards and outwards in sympathy with Nature. They have followed with their heart's delight the season of growing, blossoming and ripening, but now Nature is fading and withering. The turning-point of the year brings a crisis to human souls, who must make at this season the change from the outgoing interest of summertime to the inwardness of wintertime. They must seek within themselves the forces that give life and strength when the world around is filled with fading and decay. Man shares the life of Nature but he is not identified with it not fulfilled in its fulfilment. Within him are forces that rise and strengthen when those of Nature decline. It is imperative for him to call on these human qualities at Michaelmastime, when the outer world grows quiet and dark.

The process of turning inwards is a human experience that is not only encountered in the course of the changing seasons. Every evening the soul passes through it in some degree on the way towards sleep. The outer activities and interests of the daytime are laid aside and the soul turns to look within. When it has entirely withdrawn from the world outside, it seeks the sphere of the Spirit in sleep. The crisis of turning round meets the soul again as old age approaches. The ageing person begins of necessity to resign from outer duties. He becomes more and more absorbed in his own life of contemplation. Some people of active temperament find the change grievous and feel that they are being deprived of what is valuable in life. Yet they are in fact only changing one way of living for another just as active. They are beginning to turn away from the concerns of this world towards the experience of the world which is entered through the gate of death. They are drawing near to the great turning-point where one existence ends and another begins.

There is a touch of death in the experience of Michaelmas which reveals the true force of resurrection within the soul. As the life of Nature declines outside, the power of the Spirit rises up into consciousness within. The festival of Michaelmas is the balance and fulfilment of Easter in the course of the year. The death and resurrection of Christ, the deed of God performed on earth for the salvation of Man, is celebrated after the spring solstice. At the corresponding time in the autumn, the human soul encounters the individual experience of death from without and resurrection from within. The deed of Christ is sown in the spring and bears fruit within Mankind in the autumn. Michaelmas is a festival dedicated to the Christian ideal for human evolution. Man has not yet become what he is in truth. In earth-existence he is caught under the spell of sin and death. Christ came to release Man and lead him towards resurrection. The fulfilment of Man's true destiny at the end of time will be his rebirth in the image of Him who rose again. Each year, as Michaelmas comes round, our hearts should feel a foretaste of this ideal, through which we learn what it means to be human.

The presiding genius of Michaelmas is an archangel. He it is who goes before the heavenly hosts, leading their march through human history. All the angelic company, who send their influences into human affairs, are remembered in this festival, which is called after Michael. If Michaelmas becomes only an empty name, an essential part of world-existence is overlooked. If its true meaning is discovered again today, we shall celebrate it in honour of angels, archangels and all the company of Heaven. In this festival we recognise and acknowledge their working in our life. We human beings should grow thereby in understanding of our fellowship with them, that, instead of receiving their influences unconsciously, we may accept them knowingly and gratefully.

In the autumn season, the archangel Michael gives his aid to the human souls who are endeavouring to find the inwardness of heart appropriate to the time. In the months of late summer one may observe more frequently than at other seasons, shooting stars making their swift and shining way through the sky. From time to time one of the meteors falls down to the earth, breaking into the atmosphere with great force, scattering, where it hits the ground, lumps of meteoric iron. The virtue of the cosmic iron at work in the meteors is wielded and directed by Michael. He has dominion over the forces emanating from iron in the universe. The strength, brought to earth by the meteors, is bestowed by his hand out of the treasure of the Heavens. He is able, not only to send his gift in shooting stars from the sky, but to imbue the stream of blood flowing in human veins with the virtue of iron. Every year in the early autumn, a new force enters our blood. We notice it in a fresh touch of energy, a sharpening of interest and a sense of enterprise. This access of fresh courage comes to our aid at Michaelmastime through an invisible dew of iron strength sent by Michael out of the universe. It awakens our consciousness again after the dream of summer, which is fraught with a number of dangers for human souls. Unconscious urges may become destructive but Michael sends the clear sharp force of iron to rouse the conscience and strengthen courage.

This is only one of the tasks performed by this archangel. Every member of the hierarchies is distinguished by his powers and by the offices within the divine order of the universe which he undertakes. We human beings on earth live from their captivity, whether or not we recognise their gifts. Michael is active in the changing rhythm of time. He cares for the autumnal season in the course of the year and, at intervals, directs and leads longer epochs of history. Periods lasting three hundred years come in due turn under his dominion. Six other beings of the same rank as he have like offices and take each other's places as each epoch finishes. Our present century falls in an age which is led by Michael. When he has completed his time, he will be followed by the archangel Oriphiel. The different natures of the angelic regents give a distinct character to the epochs over which they reign. The age of Michael is dramatic, full of crisis and decision. What long lay hidden and implicit, becomes manifest on the surface. The work of the beings of evil and the healing work of the servants of Christ can be clearly apprehended.

Our thoughts turn at Michaelmastime to the Book of the Revelation of St John. There the history of the world is described, past, present and future, in visions of universal proportions. What kind of history is this? At the outset we read that John received the revelation from God at the hand of an angel. It is not the history of what individual people or even races of people have done or suffered. Neither does it speak of forces, of the development and decline of epochs, of cause becoming effect and effect bringing forth cause. The background to what is described in the Apocalypse is the wide universe itself. The span of time is the whole of earth's evolution. Those who carry out history of this order are not human beings alone. Angels, archangels and all the company of Heaven appear in the visions of St John, weaving their influences into the tapestry of evolution, moving through time and space, working each his part in the universal will of God. The Apocalypse is history in which all creatures of the Heavens and the earth are engaged, in which the veil dividing them has been torn apart, that we may behold man's life as the work of the sons of God. World-events are not caused by human action alone, nor are they the product of dark, impersonal forces. Angels and all the beings of God pour out their working in the progress of Man's evolution, into the vast drama of creation, the fall into sin and death, redemption and resurrection. The archangel is at the present time our guide to history in this sense. He opens our eyes to see and, if we will, to understand how it is made neither by the will of humans alone, nor by the urge of forces, but by the intervention of angels and the creative willing of the great gods, who exercise dominion within the universal will of the Father in the Heavens.

Michael is the archangel who faces the dragon. He confronts the power of those spiritual beings, who work evil and who try to force human souls to follow their aims. The drama of history is the struggle between the powers who serve the goodness of God and those who strive for the purposes of evil. The world of earth is the place where the drama is enacted. Human souls are the fellows of the angels in the struggle. Michael is the leader and helper in the conflict. He endows our heart with courage. He calls on us to take notice of the beings who work evil, to recognise their temptations and to understand their aims. He rouses the forces of conscience and kindles the flame of enthusiasm in those who are willing to follow him. He asks of them the heroic qualities of the heart and those who dare to respond are inspired with the ideal of what Man can become in the striving for spiritual freedom.

Michael is distinct from other angels and archangels in that, more than any other, he is close to Christ. So close is he that he is called His countenance. He moves through changing history before His face, shielding with this sternness the divine compassion of Him, whom he serves. Human hearts who can face his serious aspect are purged of weak sentiment, so that they can behold with pure eyes the loving presence of the Saviour. Michael is changing at the present time the particular way in which he works. Archangels grow and change from age to age, as, in the human sphere, people progress from experience to experience. He has at all times withstood the dragon of evil. He now continues this task, but more powerfully and clearly than ever before, he summons the souls of men and women to behold and understand the deed of Christ. Earlier he appeared as the warrior archangel, the champion against the adversary and the captain of the heavenly hosts. He still retains this office, but with the difference that another has become equally important to him. First among the beings of the Divine World to understand the deed of salvation, he now proclaims it to Mankind. He stands before us today as the herald, as the one who summons human hearts to see and to understand what took place on Golgotha. He guards the mystery, revealing it at the same time. His world-work, his angelic task, is to help Mankind to understand and absorb Christianity. At Michaelmas our thoughts turn to him, acknowledging the heavenly leader, who would guide us into the truth of Him, before whose face he stands.

THE PARABLE OF THE
MARRIAGE FEAST

The inner experience of Michaelmas is set forth in a number of parables recorded in the Gospels during the last period of the life of Jesus Christ. Such a one is the story of the marriage-feast of the king's son in the twenty-second chapter of St Matthew. Its theme is the sending out and receiving of an invitation. It is typical of all the parables that describe the coming of a great event, the striking of the crucial hour in human history. Such pictures are related to the visions unrolled in the Revelation of St John. They are among the apocalyptic passages to be found woven into the narrative of the Gospels. At Michaelmas our thoughts turn naturally to such parts of the New Testament in which the mysteries of past, present and future stand revealed in pictures that embrace the universe. At this season we lift up our human minds to contemplate the evolving of the world as it is seen in the mind of God. How can we even attempt to do this? The means for making the attempt is offered to us in just those passages of the New Testament that can be termed apocalyptic. They are revelations of the mind of God, through which we can, in flashes of insight, transcend our merely human point of view and behold the divine pattern of evolution.

Like all parables, this particular one of the marriage-feast is told dramatically, with fine economy of words and pictures. The inner meaning is expressed as much in what is omitted as in what is said. The theme of the story is a decision made in the kingdom of Heaven. At the outset the figure of a king is introduced, who resolves to make a marriage for his son. The king represents the kingdom of Heaven. His son is to be united in marriage to the bride. The figures of the bride and bridegroom remain mysteriously hidden behind the scenes from beginning to end. They never appear in the foreground. On the surface, it might even be argued that it would make no difference to the drama as it stands if the invitation had been for another kind of feast. But experience shows that the parables never unveil their meaning unless every word is given its own value. The clue to this story actually lies hidden in the bare statement that the feast is the celebration of the marriage of the king's son.

The king sends out his invitations to the guests. Servants are despatched to bid them come. There is no response. Apparently none of those invited honour the invitation. The king sends out other servants with an urgent message that all preparations for the feast have been made. The guests hear the invitation, but they do not take it seriously. Some are occupied with their work, the one with his farm, another with his business. They stand for two forms of human occupation in earthly affairs. The farmer works with what Nature gives to human beings. The merchant is busy with what humans make of the products of the earth among themselves. The whole economic sphere of life is represented in these two pictures. These guests are too preoccupied to answer the invitation. Others, who are also invited, behave differently. They turn on the servants with violence and slay them. In consequence, the king orders his armies to destroy them and their city. The host shows his power to do justice on the guests who behave like enemies. They receive what they have given without provocation.

What will the king do now? Will he abandon the marriage-feast? Will he force the preoccupied people to attend? Will he hold the marriage in his own court, among his faithful servants, and stop inviting guests who are either uninterested or hostile?

He finds still another solution. He sends out the servants again. The first guests, the privileged people of the correct standing to be invited, have not been worthy. Now the invitation is thrown open to everyone who goes up and down on the highways of life. The picture made by the words of the parable at this point suggests that all the world is to be invited. The servants are not only to go into the streets of the king's city but beyond the gates to the roads that lead into the country, where the strangers come and go. No more distinctions are to be made between friend and stranger, not even between good people and bad. The rogues are summoned along with the good-living folk. There is no lack of response now. The feast is crowded with guests.

The main event, the marriage itself, is not included in the picture. The parable is concerned with the host and the guests. When they are assembled, the king comes in to join them. How is this scene to be imagined? Has the feast become a charity-meal given by a rich ruler to the stragglers and down-and-outs, instead of a banquet for his noble folk, who would not bestir themselves to come? So it would appear, until we see how the king behaves. One man is without the wedding garment. The guests have to be dressed in a suitable fashion, as if they were of the same standing as those who would not come. There is, however, no sign that the king asked anything unreasonable of those he invited. Some commentators believe that, in the background of this scene, is an oriental custom by which the host provided garments for the guests at a feast. The king addresses the man who is not clad for the wedding in a manner that would do him honour. He does not speak to him as if he had disobeyed orders, refused to conform to the regulations, or been too careless to dress like the others. He turns to him as to a respectable person and asks him, why? The king has clearly expected that those who are invited from the highways will, to use a somewhat inadequate expression, rise to the occasion. Each one is capable of becoming a guest to whom the king can say "friend". The wedding-garment has not been intended to cover up the fact that the people invited are not really royal guests but can be made to appear so for the occasion. Each one present has been expected to call upon something in himself for which the garment is a worthy expression. In wearing the robe he has become a king's companion, able to exchange question and answer with him.

The man without the garment has not found the inner capacity to wear it. He has certainly not been expected to come to the feast in clothes he would be too poor to possess. He has been expected to appear in the status of a true guest, which he should have been able to achieve. It lies with himself that he fails. The next part of the story makes this quite clear. He cannot answer the king's question. He is speechless. He not only is without the garment, he cannot behave as a guest and speak to the king. The consequence follows immediately. The invitation had been openly and freely given, but it is not to be accepted without responsibility and even risk on the part of the guests. The king calls his servants to throw out the man, binding him hand and foot and casting him into the darkness outside where the soul can experience only grief and lamentation.

The story culminates in a riddle that is harder to solve from sentence to sentence. It is to be understood only by finding the clue to the secret in the fact that the royal son's marriage is being celebrated. The king is the kingdom of Heaven and the guests are the human souls on earth. The bridegroom is the Son of God. The Father has resolved that the time has come for the Son's union with the bride. He invites human souls to take part in the celebration of the spiritual marriage, of the binding together of that which has been separate. Once, at the turn of time, the Son of God was sent by the kingdom of Heaven to seek that which was lost on earth. Christ came to unite Himself with Mankind in the world that had been separated from the Divine by the Fall into evil. Such is the mystery hidden in this parable. The Father has decided to give the Son to be united with lost Mankind, and He invites the individual human souls to be witnesses of what He has resolved and will perform.

The parable faces towards the world of men, that is to say, it describes the human part in this world-event. It stresses the invitation and the behaviour of those invited. It is the king's own resolve to invite the guests. As an act of divine grace, without hint that it was desired or requested by those bidden, the message is sent. The servants are despatched without reproach a second time, when the first message was not understood. The king gives freely of his grace. The second messengers are so powerful that their bidding is heard and understood. The invited ones now have a choice. At this moment in the drama only certain people are called. How is the choice made? In the past, especially in the earlier half of history, the connection between the divine and human worlds was maintained through the great leaders of the different races of people. As long as religion was not yet a matter of individual experience but of pious devotion to the spiritual life of the tribe or folk, leaders, whether priests or kings, stood between the people and their God. When the kingdom of Heaven resolved on the act of redemption these were the human beings whose leadership put them in the position to be first invited to receive the revelation. To them came the choice to accept or reject, to turn away to their earthly interests or even to fight against the message.

The servants of the kingdom belong to the angelic company of Heaven. To realise this alters the whole character of the retribution suffered by those who maltreat the messengers. The spiritual servants visit human souls from within, not only from without. The one who refuses to listen to the message his own angel speaks in his heart does harm to himself, shuts his soul off from inspiration by his own will. Anyone who goes further and attacks the divine voice within, throws the messenger violently from him, destroys something in his own human nature. The king's vengeance is not in reality an attack from outside. The soul chooses to destroy the higher part within itself.

When those first invited have refused, the kingdom of Heaven makes a new decision. The invitation is thrown open to all human souls without distinction. Each one has his own connection with the Spirit and hears his call. The time of the leaders is over. No condition is made. All may approach the marriage-feast, both bad and good. Nevertheless, once the guests have entered, a distinction arises from out of themselves. One guest is not prepared for the revelation. He is unable to speak, he feels himself thrown out. An analogy from daily life, inadequate as it is, throws light on what happens. Everyone who can buy a ticket can go to a concert, but when it begins there is a great difference among the people present. An unmusical person may feel that he is in the wrong place, that he is shut out from what his neighbours are hearing and understanding. He may suffer considerably from his sense of insufficiency. So it is with the man who has no wedding-garment. The servants who turn him out are within him. He begins to recognise that he is not only speechless but unable to move his limbs. He feels himself shut out, and the pain of not being able to receive what is offered begins to torment him. But pain is a process of becoming aware of something wrong. The grief described in the parable as wailing and gnashing of teeth is the sign of hope for this unhappy guest. In the darkness, he begins to awaken in longing for the revelation he could not receive. The opportunity is offered to waken through grief and to change himself into a guest who is able to be present when he is admitted to the marriage. The outlook is not hopeless for him. The future is not yet closed. The situation lies with himself, so the parable ends of necessity unfinished.

The working of Christ in the world of earth is revealed in human souls time and time again. In a true communion-service at the altar, in prayer and meditation, in the great experiences of a lifetime, in many ways, His revelation is offered to us. We are invited to the marriage-feast, to celebrate His union with Mankind, by the grace of the Divine World. Nevertheless, there is responsibility on our side. It depends on our readiness in heart and mind whether we truly take part. Both the good and the bad are invited, but the difference between being good or bad guests is of the greatest importance. The distinction is not made in the invitation but arises in the accepting of the guest's place. The grace of the king asks for recognition, which we can give only out of our moral responsibility. Our part is to become capable of wearing the wedding-garment, of speaking and moving in the royal presence.

This parable and the others of the same pattern speak of our human part in the divine act of salvation performed by the Father and the Son. They are a summons to wakefulness and responsibility. The archangel of the autumn season, Michael, speaks the same message to our hearts and offers us his special grace of courage to hear the call. At Michaelmas these parables remind us through their pictures of that for which we should be listening at this festival.

THE SIGN IN HEAVEN

The Book of the Revelation of St John lays open in lofty visions the history of the future. In the season of Michaelmas and in the weeks that follow, our thoughts turn naturally to the pictures of things to come which we find in the last book of the Bible. We strain our inner eyes towards the future and the world's end in order to illumine the meaning of the present. We look for the answer to the last question: Man, whither goest thou? Whether the answer is found depends very much on how the mysterious pictures are read, in which the prophecies of the New Testament are clothed. In no sense do they represent foregone conclusions, a predestined course of events from which there is no escape, a relentless fate bearing down upon Mankind. The destiny of the world is not arranged on such lines. It could be truly described as a work of art, unfinished, still being evolved, of which the Divine World is the artist, who summons human beings to become fellow-workers. The evolution of the world is not set in unalterable shape. It grows and becomes in the evolving, but not in a loose and purposeless fashion. The direction is given by the aims of God. World-destiny is consecrated to ideals and purposes that live and work in the heart of God and inspire the becoming of His artistic creation. In calling upon Humanity to work with Him, he has shared the divine aims with human souls in revelations, of which that received by St John is the pattern. When we look at the world-pictures of the Apocalypse, we behold the divine ideas for evolution and share the foresight of God. Whether we understand what we see or not depends on how far our minds can penetrate into the divine mind.

In the twelfth chapter of the Book of the Revelation the mystery of evolution is expressed in a picture, of which the Archangel Michael is the most active figure. If the attempt is now made to interpret the signs depicted in this passage, it is not with the pretence of making a final explanation. It is with the aim of trying to grasp something of the significance of this vision with the thinking of today. Each person can make such experiments in understanding for himself with any or all of the pictures from the Apocalypse. This one attempt may be considered as a starting-point for many others, for which there is too little space here.

The first of the signs in this chapter is the woman seen in the Heavens, clothed with the sun, crowned with twelve stars, standing upon the moon. She is a picture from the universe, a goddess whose dwelling is the cosmos itself. The sun is her heart and its beams surround her with a garment of light. The moon has no domination over her, but she can support herself on the groundwork of its ancient forces. The twelve star-pictures, which circle the earth and are called the Zodiac, are the crowd round her head. They send forth and interchange their influences, weaving a starry garland across the sky. She appears in the Heavens, a goddess in whom the forces of the universe are concentrated. The soul of the world appears in a divine female form. She is the queen of Heaven, the Madonna who has not yet descended to the earth. Nevertheless, the heavenly forces surrounding her work down upon human beings. Mankind is created in the reflection of the stars and planets by which she lives. We look up in thought to her image in the universe and behold there the origin of that which we find in ourselves.

An event is taking place among the signs in Heaven. A child is about to be born to the woman. A divine birth is at hand, a new stage of creation is to begin. At that moment the Adversary comes upon the scene, the great red dragon with seven heads, ten horns and seven crowns. He acts as destroyer and disturber. He takes part of the stars and throws them down to earth. The divine order is deranged. The inhabitants of the earthly world receive forces which have their right function among the stars. He waits before the woman to destroy the child. The new birth shall not come to its fulfilment in the universe. It is threatened with destruction by the great beast. How does he come into the picture? He also belongs to the universe. His features, heads, horns and crowns, represent cosmic powers, but they have been turned by his dragon-nature into the opposite of the influences which bring about harmony and creation. The Heavens have their opposites, the beings who work evil, whose will is set against the divine order of evolution. The red dragon brings evil upon the cosmic scene. He acts as the devouring beast who would destroy that which is to be born.

The hour of birth has come. A man-child is brought forth in the Heavens. He is destined to be the leader of the new age of evolution. He will go before all nations and the sign of his leadership is to be a staff of iron. A fresh quality is to be made available through his coming. The iron virtue of will, held with conscious resolve in the hand, wielded with courage, is the gift which he can bestow. He appears upon the scene of the universe as the newborn son, the male figure proceeding from the female being who was seen first in the vision. The Heavens are ripe for the new time when the World-Mother brings forth the World-Son in the sphere of the light-giving sun. Therewith the sun changes his nature. He has radiated quickening light, giving to the wide world the power of life, nourishing with the pure forces of creation all living things. Henceforth another virtue lives in the spiritual essence of the sun. The Man-child represents the living power of egohood. To be capable of bearing a self, awake and responsible, having will of one's own to wield in the service of world-ideals, is the meaning of this power. It was born into the universe before it descended into human souls to become there the true force of spiritual individuality. Egohood is known to our experience only in its humanised form, but when we lift our thoughts to the heights of the world we find its origin in the sphere of the sun. Its first revelation was the cosmic act of birth described in the vision of the Man-child.

The dragon is not able to reach the child, because he is taken up to the throne of God, but the woman has to escape from her place in the Heavens and to withdraw into loneliness. Thereupon a new drama opens in the universe. Battle begins with the dragon, under the leadership of Michael. The Heavens are filled with struggle against the adversaries of the divine order. It ends with the dragon being thrown out of the heights down into the earth. The spheres of Heaven are purified of his presence, but the earth must receive him.

In a clear, simple picture the twelfth chapter of Revelation describes the world-mystery of evil. How does the Divine World act towards the adversaries, the beings who are the bearers of evil? There is struggle in Heaven: the dragon does not prevail, but neither is he destroyed. He is thrown down into the earth. The ultimate solution of the problem of evil is not shown in the twelfth chapter. Nevertheless one fact is stressed there. The earthly world is the place where it is to be worked out for the sake of the whole universe. God is solving the problem of evil among us human beings, who dwell on earth. The visions of this chapter do not contain the human point of view. They describe the mind of God. We who read them are faced with the question: why should the dragon be banished into the life of human beings of earth?

The earthly world has become separate from the Divine World. At the beginning it was not so. The great event of the Fall of Man, the interference with creation by the serpent of evil, brought about the separation. The earth became material and fell into the power of death. Mankind became involved with the existence of this world in its separate state, in its estrangement from the life of the Heavens. In the entire universe the sphere of the earth became an exception, a negative place where the divine order persisted only as a memory. Yet this world is not without its purpose. Released from the compelling control of the divine order, the life of human souls provides the place where the beings of evil are at liberty to follow their own intentions. In the visions of this chapter the devil is shown in the form of the dragon. The picture is a composite one, including within it the two opposing princes of evil and the beings of lesser dignity who serve them. The hardened bony form of the beast indicates the force of evil that would drag everything further and further into materialisation, into a fixed, cold state and ultimately into death. The pull downwards is known to everyone as an inner experience of the soul. It is the temptation to grasp the world intellectually, to see it as an arrangement of mechanical forces, to treat material appearance as the only reality. This part of the dragon's nature is expressed in his lust to disturb and destroy. The other aspect of his nature is expressed by his colour, red, and his great tail that lashes out among the stars. He shows in these features the opposite force of evil, that would dissolve everything away upwards into unreality. The pull away upwards is as familiar to everyone from within as is its opposite. It is felt in the temptation to be swayed by passionate emotions, to escape into the spheres of wishful thinking. The hot wrath of the dragon expresses this part of his character. The influences of evil stream from the two opposite directions and they exercise a double pull in the life of the soul. The human being finds the good active within him in creating the balance between the two opposing forces.

We know the power of the dragon from our inner experience of soul. He is a real being, who plays a part in the drama of the universe. The twelfth chapter goes on to describe what comes about when the dragon has arrived on earth. He discovers there the woman who has borne the child. She has likewise left the spheres of the Heavens and, goddess as she is, has descended earthwards. Here, in this separated world, is her wilderness. The dragon, having lost the child, pursues the mother. She is lifted by eagles' wings out of his reach. All human souls are graced with the gifts of this heavenly mother, the Madonna whom the angels acknowledge as queen. A treasure of innocence is still preserved in them, in spite of the struggle with the twofold forces of temptation. The goddess is hidden in a place of loneliness. She does not go back to the Heavens but the dragon cannot reach her. Not only the eagles' wings from above rescue her, another help comes from below. The earth herself opens to swallow up the flood of water from the dragon's mouth, which threatened her. The earth is likewise born of the Gods, a divine creation though she has come under the spell of matter. She understands how to help the heavenly mother in her need. Then the dragon is left to struggle with the offspring of the woman in this world, that is to say with the human souls who derive their nature from their heavenly origin. Human life on earth becomes the place in the universe in which is evolved the mystery of evil.

The twelfth chapter does not take the story beyond this point. The sequel is written in the history of the world itself. Before leaving this vision, we should look at what emerges from the great cosmic event which it describes. The child, who was caught up to God, came in due time down to earth, into the realm over which the dragon had become prince. Another great birth took place, not in the Heavens but on earth. The Madonna bore the child over whom the star of Christ shone. The dragon was again at hand, but he did not prevail until the hour of Golgotha. Thereby he met face to face in his own kingdom of death the One, who had the strength to overcome him. When Christ came down to the world of man on earth, He brought with Him the power that had been born earlier in the universe, through the great birth among sun, moon and stars described in the vision. True egohood became Christ's gift to Man. It had been evolved in the Heavens and was now to be realised on earth. The capacity to become a self out of the Spirit allows Mankind to make fruitful the struggle with the dragon. True freedom, a quality not known elsewhere in the wide universe, can evolve in human souls which can face through true selfhood the power of evil. The birth of the divine child among human beings will be fulfilled when a picture of Man will become true which still belongs to the future. One day Man should be seen clothed in light, as the divine mother was seen apparelled in the sun, with the dragon under his feet. When free spiritual activity streams like sunlight from the heart of Man, under his feet, giving him the support on which he can stand, will be found the power of the dragon. The birth in the Heavens has taken place. The vision of it is the promise that the power is created, and is present with us on earth in Christ, through which the future picture of Man can be realised. Michael has cast the dragon down to this world, but the strength of the child begotten in the Heavens is given to human souls, that out of their freedom the bringer of evil shall find his true place under the feet of Man, who has been transformed by the Spirit.

THE BELOVED CITY

The great visions of the Book of the Revelation stretch away to the horizon, where the world ends. They call on us to widen our powers of imagination until we can see with understanding that which they reveal of the ultimate aims of our existence. When we think of the future, we are inclined to say: what next? This is too short-sighted for the Book of the Revelation, which takes the long view, requiring the question: what is the true aim and end of human life on earth? The close of the Christian year, which falls between Michaelmas and Advent, is a time when a particular effort should be made to look into the far distances of the future. When the ultimate things are brought into the consciousness of the present, they illumine the struggle of today with the light of the ideal ahead. When passing from the experience of one year's round to the next, it is of the greatest value to look beyond the immediate concerns and see them absorbed into the whole stream of evolution. Truly, we have to live a year at a time, a day and even a minute at a time, but as each passes its worth flows into the future, widening and helping to make real the aims of world-existence.

Two pictures appear as the visions seen by St John unfold, which flower in the closing chapters of the book with the revelation of the ultimate end. The one is of a city, the new Jerusalem, and its shadow opposite. Babylon, which goes to destruction. The other is of the mystical marriage. The bride and bridegroom appear one moment quite clearly, then another picture rises and obscures them. Again they are in the foreground, seen somewhat differently, only to disappear as the vision moves and changes. Even in the last chapter of the book, when they are seen quite distinctly and the reader expects to know at last who and what they are, another picture rolls like a cloud across them, leaving them a mystery, seen and yet not seen. The last visions of St John intermingle so much that these two themes, that of the holy city and that of the mystical marriage, finally flow together. To the ordinary imagination this is inconceivable. It sounds like a grotesquely mixed metaphor. However, the Book of the Revelation does not deal in metaphors but in visions, which rise, develop, grow and change with the realities they represent. The ultimate mystery of existence is hidden in the flowing together of these two so diverse pictures. Without attempting to interpret them, for they express their own meaning best as they stand in the wording of the New Testament, we may try to unlock their secret.

Let us begin by tracing the parable of the mystical marriage, which appears both in the Gospels and in the Book of the Revelation again and again before the closing scene. The story is not told all at once, but in scattered passages here and there. When they are pieced together, something seems to have happened to the picture between one fragment and the next. The parable appears, disappears and comes to the surface again, having gone meanwhile through a hidden process of transformation. The whole is perceived not by putting the pieces together side by side but by following them one after another in time.

The picture is found first in the preaching of John the Baptist. He was asked questions about Jesus Christ by his disciples. His answer is recorded in the third chapter of St John's Gospel: "He that hath the bride is the bridegroom, but the friend of the bridegroom, who standeth and heareth him, rejoiceth greatly because of the bridegroom's voice: this my joy therefore is fulfilled."

John described Christ as the bridegroom coming to the marriage. His words are reminiscent of the legends, like that of Lohengrin, which tell of the bride in distress, to whom the mysterious bridegroom comes from another world. Unable to tell the secret of his name or his kinsfolk, he is a stranger who can bestow blessing on all around him while he can remain. His going is a tragedy caused by human weakness. The bride is too frail in character to keep the divine presence with her for more than a short time. Such a picture was used by John to describe how Christ descended from the Heavens to rescue the earthly bride, who was helpless and in danger. Who could this bride be but the soul of all Mankind, "Mansoul", to borrow an old term, who was beset by the forces of evil, the princes of this world. Christ came, not to remove Mansoul back to Paradise, to the shelter and security of the Divine World, but to unite His life with the being of Man, to take upon Himself the destiny of the less world. He came as the bridegroom, seeking marriage with the lost, weak being who was without strength to withstand the wiles of the evil ones. He offered His divine power to aid her in the struggle of earth-existence. John's insight into the destiny of man showed him the vision of the marriage. He was able to take the friend's part in the divine drama of salvation, because he could understand what was to take place. He was filled with joy, not yet seeing the tragic aspect of what was to come, but exalted with wonder at beholding the Son of God in His glory stepping down to the sad, dark earth, to call lost Mansoul to become the bride in the divine marriage.

In the fifth chapter of St Luke's Gospel, the same picture of the bridegroom hastening to the marriage is found in the words of Christ Himself, which He spoke when He was asked why His disciples did not fast. While He is with them, His followers are like guests rejoicing at the wedding-feast, was the answer. John the Baptist had the insight to see His coming in the same picture. He beheld Christ invading this darkened world and shedding upon it His divine light and joy. He saw the heavenly hero coming to rescue the maiden from the dangers of evil and calling her to become the bride.

The next development of the theme is found in two parables, told in St Matthew's Gospel among the teaching given towards the end of the life of Jesus Christ. The one is the story of the king's marriage-feast in the twenty-second chapter, and the other is of the wise and foolish virgins in the twenty-fifth. Both parables tell of the guests who are to take part in the marriage. The first says that the kingdom of Heaven is like to a king who invited guests to the wedding-feast of his son. The bride and bridegroom remain completely in the background of this scene, which describes how the invitation was sent and how the guests behaved. God Himself invites, and human souls are invited to take part in a mystery, which the guests can scarcely understand. The second parable says that the kingdom of Heaven is like ten virgins who have lamps ready to greet the bridegroom's coming. Five have oil, and five foolishly neglect to prepare the oil beforehand. When the bridegroom comes they have gone to buy what they need and on their return they find the place of the marriage shut. His voice is heard through the closed door. He is mysteriously hidden in the background of this scene, as in the first.

The stress in the earlier parable is laid on the king's act of invitation. In the later one it rests on the answer of the guests. The king who invites represents the kingdom of Heaven, but later on this is the part of the ten waiting virgins. A divine force lives and works within the guests. Are they ready to meet the heavenly bridegroom with the light of the Spirit burning strongly in their hearts? If they do not find out, until the hour for the marriage has come, that they are in want of the forces to kindle their own inner light, they will be shut out from the mystery. Each human soul can only make his own lamp to burn. The first parable points to the universal Spirit of God in the Heavens, the second to the individual Spirit enshrined in each human heart. When the great mystery of union is celebrated, in which Christ is the bridegroom, God the Father invites human beings to take part, but each one is present through the power of the Spirit within himself. Just as each person must go through death alone, just as many other experiences have to be faced with one's own inner forces, so has the invitation to the divine marriage to be answered. No one can light the lamp for another. Each soul goes to the bridegroom by virtue of that portion of the kingdom of Heaven that lives and shines within himself.

After these parables the picture of the marriage does not appear again for a long while. Then, near the end of the Revelation of St John, in the nineteenth chapter, a voice from Heaven proclaims: "the marriage of the Lamb is come". Immediately before this happens, the great vision has been unrolled of the fall of Babylon, the city of destruction, the loathly opposite to Jerusalem the city of God. When this is accomplished, a mighty psalm of praise is sung in Heaven, which is followed by the proclamation of the marriage. Can this be the same event as that of which John the Baptist and Christ Himself spoke in the Gospels?

The history of Christ in relation to Mankind is a long evolution. One great act of union has been performed by Christ already, when He became a man, went through the death on the cross, and rose again to unite Himself with the future destiny of the earthly world. That event has happened in the past, but another act of union is ahead in times to come. It is the world-aim towards which He directs earthly destiny. When the hour is come it will be proclaimed from the Heavens. The passage in chapter nineteen is a vision of the future. Here the two figures of the bride and bridegroom appear clearly in the foreground. The invitation has been sent and the vision seems to promise that now the mystery of the marriage will be performed. Just at this moment the picture changes again. John sees Heaven opened, showing him the sight of the rider on the white horse. He is the leader of the heavenly hosts and three mysterious names are to be read upon his shining form. Upon his head is the name which no one knows but himself. Over the garment coloured with blood is written: the Word of God. Still lower, upon the thigh, stands the title: King of Kings and Lord of Lords. Has the picture of the marriage disappeared? This might seem to be so, but in truth the new vision is still a part of that picture. This is the bridegroom who now appears, having written upon his garment the names of Christ.

What are these names? The first, on the head, is that which only he can speak whose name it is, that is to say, it signifies the self. True spiritual selfhood, of which Christ has charge throughout the universe, is the mystery of the presence of God within each single soul. No one can name this for another. He must evoke it from himself, from that which lives within him. On the head of the bridegroom is written the name of self-knowledge. On the garment stands the title: Word of God. Christ is He who has created the world. At the beginning, the divine substance of the Godhead was poured forth. Out of the divine silence the Word of God spoke in the act of creation. The Son manifested the nature of God the Father, in whom the world-substance of creation exists. The garment of the rider on the white horse is woven of the forces that move and flow throughout the created world. Just as the earth wears the garment of Nature, so the rider wears the clothing prepared by that which lives and weaves as Nature in the whole universe. What the stars distil as their essences of life is the stuff of which it is made, but the whole has been dipped and coloured in blood. The influence of the deed of the cross on Golgotha has changed what is given by the stars from above. The mark of the earth has been put on the garment.

The third name, King of Kings and Lord of Lords, is seen on the thigh, which represents the limbs as the instruments of will and action. In the place of thinking, on the head, the name of self-knowledge is written. In the centre of feeling, round the heart, is found the name which comprehends the weaving forces of creation in the star-filled universe. In the region of the willing on the limbs, stands the name of self-will. The king over whom no other ruler has authority, the lord who is above all lords, directs his will out of himself. No other can deserve such a title but the true self who, known above in the head, has power of action below in the limbs. Such a will is centred in itself, determining its activity through the responsibility of the self, offering its power to serve in self-sacrifice the world-aims of God. True self-will matures in the one who is king over the forces within his nature and lord of his aims and purposes, because they are not bred from self-interest but from devotion to the divine destiny of the world.

The rider is Christ, revealing in Himself the original of the Christian force we can find reflected within our own human souls. True selfhood has its origin with Him in the universe. When He says "I", the world's power of knowledge and will through the self speaks in Him. He brought to earth the essence of true godlike selfhood, and sows it as spiritual seed in the field of mankind. The seed was grown and ripened in the Heavens. In the time to come it should bring forth a new harvest on earth. The vision of Christ at this moment in the revelation of St John, when the bridegroom is awaited, reveals Him in the heights of the universe as the One who knows within Himself the world-power that can speak: "I am that I am." Although St John sees this picture in the Heavens, it expresses what Christ has become through His being man on earth, by going through death and achieving resurrection. Such a vision could not have been seen before Golgotha. He is transformed since that event in the sight of God. His new appearance before the angels, archangels and all the company of Heaven is beheld by the seer as he looks for the coming of the promised bridegroom.

The rider on the white horse represents Christ as He bears into the drama of world-evolution that which has evolved within His being through the deed of death and life on earth. In place of the long-awaited vision of the marriage, the scene which follows describes the last great battle with the powers of evil. They are finally overcome, in the sense that they are held fast and confined to the places in the universe where their nature can uphold, instead of breaking down, the divine order. Thereupon the souls of men and women must encounter the last judgement. Of all creatures in the world, they alone are not fixed and finished by force of natural laws. They are free to determine what they shall become. In the final crisis they face the test, which shows what they have made of themselves. Have they followed the way of evolution towards life, or have they taken part in the trend that goes towards destruction and world-death? At the last, the final test must be faced and each one gathers the harvest of his own existence.

When the ultimate conflict is ended, the clouds of wrath clear away and another vision rises before the gaze of St John. The new and holy city descends from Heaven, prepared as a bride going to meet her husband. Once more the bride, whose picture was so long overclouded, is seen in her glory. How much she has changed since the parable first began in the Gospels. She is no longer the frail, distressed maiden, Mansoul upon earth. She comes down from God, hallowed and renewed in all her being. The changing scenes of the last visions of St John's revelation show no final portrait of the bridegroom, and yet he is revealed from different sides through all the varied pictures of the two closing chapters. When the bride now appears from above, He comes from below. The working of Christ in Mankind on earth will so transform human nature in those who seek to follow Him that men and women will become resurrected in His image. When the true self reigns within human hearts, the soul-nature of men and women will be healed and renewed by the heavenly forces of God. Sick souls will be purified and strengthened by the power of the Spirit. Mansoul, transformed by the Christian process of salvation, will become the true bride of the heavenly bridegroom, who has taken upon Himself the destiny of the earth.

Then the vision of the holy city will become a world-reality. The city, lighted from within by the light of God and of the Lamb, is Man resurrected in body, soul and spirit. That which the body gives to our eternal soul will not be lost at the great transformation. It will suffer a spiritual change, and its redeemed forces will give firm shape and foundation to the spiritual being of Man, The Spirit of redeemed Mankind is Christ, the soul is the bride coming down from God, the body is the heavenly city. When the bride and bridegroom are united, the vision must of inner necessity transform itself into the picture of the city of God, New Jerusalem. The community of Mankind, resurrected from the death of earth-existence into life in the world of God, is the city, whose indwelling light is Christ.

Step by step, day by day, we tread our portion of the great road of human destiny. We strain our eyes to see where it leads, where it will end. It is not hard to observe that much in our world will cease in death. Those who know that Christ is with us see further. Beyond the shadows of death, they perceive the dawn of new life. St John saw it through the vision of the bride, the bridegroom and the holy city. Such a picture can show its true meaning to all who contemplate it in their heart. They, who grow to understand it, will say: there is light at the end of the road for those who love the light.

ON CELEBRATING FESTIVALS

ON CELEBRATING FESTIVALS

The course of the Christian festivals is a path of spiritual experience leading through the round of the year. We may take the path in our inner life by contemplating at each season the appropriate part of the Christian revelation and by following the festivals in the services of any Christian church. In earlier times, when what was sacred and secular was less sharply divided than it is today, the festivals of the year were also marked by customs commonly observed in outer life. A few of these still survive in a highly commercialised form. The shops advertise presents for Christmas and eggs for Easter. Long ago, a wise but instinctive insight made people realise that the round of daily life should be hallowed and beautified by the customs derived from the recurring festivals. Although such observances have in the true sense lapsed, many people are beginning, out of their modern understanding, to look for ways of bringing back a hallowing influence of a similar kind into the everyday routine. Some old customs can well be revived, because new meaning is to be found in them. New ones may be discovered by the power of imagination which is fostered by contemplating the inner meaning of the different festivals. Some suggestions along these lines will follow, which are simple to carry out in practice, but they will by no means exhaust the subject.

Advent

In Advent the Christian year begins. A suitable token for this season is the wreath, which by its round shape represents the circle of the year. It is usually made of fir branches, but any similar evergreen may be used. When the green twigs have been fastened to a ring made of a dry stick bound together at the ends, the wreath is ready to be decorated with red ribbon and four candles. They are to be lighted one for each Sunday leading to Christmas, so that all four burn only on the fourth Sunday of Advent. The wreath may be hung or placed in a prominent position in the house or in the room, and the candles may be lit each evening. Pictures are an important part in the celebration of Advent. Those which show the holy Mother with the Child are the most suitable, to be replaced at Christmas by those which describe the scene of the Nativity. Children especially like to have an Advent calendar. This is composed of a number of little windows, one for each day from the first Advent Sunday until Christmas Eve, behind which tiny pictures are hidden. Each morning or evening, the little shutters of one window are opened, until on Christmas Eve the largest, last window alone remains. A sheet of cardboard or paper is sufficient to contain all the windows, if they are small, and a second sheet pasted on behind provides space for all the tiny pictures to be painted. Once a window is opened, it is not shut again, so that, as Advent continues, more and more pictures appear. Their subjects should be such that they can become part of the final picture of the Mother with the Child.

Christmas

Singing carols rightly belongs to Advent and Christmas. The realm of Nature has grown still and quiet in the winter. Inside the houses, people begin to sing of His coming, who brought the light into the world's darkness. The old custom that people went from house to house singing Christmas carols was a proper expression of what the souls experienced at this festival. Today we need to find a new feeling for the true meaning of human voices sounding in the dark, quiet wintertime. Little children readily understand this, if they are taught to sing for a short time each evening before going to bed, beside the wreath with its lighted candles. The caricature that carol-singing has often become need not spoil its right value.

Lighting candles is one of the essential joys of Advent and Christmas time. The little flame spurts up in the darkness and the waxy body of the candle is consumed bit by bit in the activity of making light. No amount of coloured electric light bulbs can replace real candles, which speak the language of the Spirit as they consume themselves in burning. Naturally they should, for safety's sake, be watched while they burn, but watching them is part of the Christian experience. In the weeks of Advent the decorations may be prepared that will be at their best for the time of the Holy Nights. Evergreen branches, pictures and candles are the most important items, with golden, silver and coloured stars hung about them if one wishes for more. The world within doors should blossom with lighted candles and coloured pictures as Christmas approaches. Cards sent with good wishes by friends may enhance the scene in the house, if they add to the wealth of good pictures. The everyday appearance of the rooms should be covered up by their Christmas clothing and decorations of every kind should express something of the festival's significance. A candle may stand on a piece of wood cut into the shape of a five-pointed star. Then, when alight, it is a token of the flame of the human Spirit burning in the body, which has, when arms and legs are outstretched, the form of a star with five points. Another candle may stand on a red apple. This again represents the light of the Spirit in the house of the body.

Another significant piece of decoration may be made with paper and a glass jar. Petals are cut out of red paper and leaves of green. They are pasted round the jar and a night-light is put inside. When it is lighted, the whole is a red rose, shining from the light within. In summer the roses will blossom in the sun's light without. At midwinter the mystical rose shines with the Spirit's light from within the human heart. Old and new customs of a similar kind may be found to help transform the scenery of daily life.

The tree is the favourite centrepiece of all decoration. The dark fir was originally brought into church and house during Advent as the symbol of Man's fall into sin through the eating of forbidden fruit. It was used, and can still be so used today, for the performance of a folk-play about the sin of Adam and Eve, to be followed by plays of the Nativity. At Christmas it should change its appearance, receiving the flowers it lacked before. Candles are lighted on its dark branches, and between them are hung signs depicting the shining planets in the Heavens. Roses, either living or artificial ones, may also be added, in number corresponding to the years of the life of Jesus Christ on earth. So the tree will be changed from a symbol of the Fall into a sign of Man's salvation, at the festival of His birth.

The presents which people give to each other at Christmas time are symbols of the original gift of His Son to people on earth by the Father in the Heavens. True sense can be found in the custom, if its meaning is remembered. When little children hang up their stockings to be filled by the invisible Father Christmas, they are following a rite started in honour of the divine gift. The fathers and mothers who actually put in the treasures represent the divine Father on that night, and their presents are tokens of that which we all receive to nourish us from the Heavens above. Gifts may also be placed round the decorated tree, but beneath its branches the picture of the Nativity should have the centre place. Little figures of wood or plaster are often made to represent Mary, Joseph and the shepherds, who are grouped in the stable round a light, which stands for the new-born child. Sometimes other figures are added to the scene. In many villages it used to be the custom to include all the different craftsmen and workers of the community in the gathering at the crib of the Christ child and to surround the stable with a familiar landscape. People said of themselves in so doing: He is born among us now. In this sense, it is good when a scene of this kind is prepared in each house during Advent, even if it is artistically primitive.

Epiphany

The tree with its picture of the Nativity may remain in the room until January 6th, when the Holy Nights end. The festival of the Three Kings then begins. Another scene of the Nativity should replace the one made for Christmas. Instead of the shepherds, the kings should be shown, and in place of the stable the background should be a house, something like a palace. The tree will be gone, but over the whole scene a great star should hang, surrounded, if it is wished, by representations of angels. This picture may be kept for the four weeks of Epiphany in a place prepared in the corner of the room. Most of the decorations will disappear after the end of the Holy Nights, but the stars should remain. Special stars may be made, to be kept through the weeks of the winter that now follow, as a reminder that the light of Christmas has entered human hearts, to shine there through the coming year. The celebration of Christmas should not end in an abrupt return to the ways of ordinary life. Epiphany should be so kept that, as Christmas passes, it fades, not away, but into the inner place of our souls. We no longer see the picture of Christmas in the rooms of the house, but we look to the star as the token of the Spirit's light shining upon our ways throughout the year.

Lent

The group of festivals that follow next come in the spring. Lent, the period of preparation for Easter, is the season in which the contrast is experienced between the fresh, budding life in Nature and the weakness and poverty which the human soul finds in itself. The inner being is revived, not by the natural vitality of springtime, but by the awakening of the Spirit within. In earlier times a particular style of living was considered appropriate to Lent. People practised fasting, with the aim of controlling the vital forces and preserving a sober mood in the soul, and the repentant contemplation of their sins and weaknesses, in the hope of achieving a better moral condition. In the present time Lent still offers the opportunity for living differently, but modern people require not fasting but the more positive effort of undertaking tasks of a spiritual nature, deliberately chosen, without the compulsion of necessity. It is good to observe Lent by setting aside a space of time each day to do something outside the usual routine. There are books one has long wished to study, a particular spiritual exercise not yet attempted, or even a subject one intends to learn about that has never been started. Children may be encouraged to begin making or learning something new, with the aim of being finished by Easter. Calling in this manner on the force of one's own soul is a more effective form of self-discipline than the old kind of repentance and penance.

On Palm Sunday there is a custom of making and distributing small crosses formed from a frond of palm leaf. They may serve as a symbol for the time of Holy Week, but pictures representing scenes from the events of Easter are quite as helpful. A quiet, concentrated mood in daily life is valuable throughout the week between Palm Sunday and Easter Day. In churches special Lenten addresses are frequently held at this time. Some people may find it easier to enter into the mood of Easter by attending such gatherings held outside one's own home. Others may prefer to fill by themselves the time they can make free for contemplation. The old way of religious experience was to follow in feeling and imagination the outer stages of Christ's passion and death. Today it is necessary for us to deepen our understanding and widen our conception of Christ's coming, His deed on Golgotha and His resurrection. We have less need to consider the outer pictures and more to strive after the inner significance of what took place. It is not wise to introduce children too far into such contemplations before they have developed the powers of soul which can only mature after the age of fourteen. Before that time they should look at the events of Christ's life in pictures seen from outside, somewhat in imitation of the old way of experience. It will be helpful to them to share in the quiet, thoughtful mood made during these days by the older people.

Easter

Easter is the festival of joy in the Resurrection and of hopeful courage for the future destiny of the world. When the Christ-given Spirit wakens within the soul, human beings share with full hearts the earth's joy of spring. Lent has been a period of contemplation and of inner activity. At Easter the soul turns to meet the world without through the inner strength that, uniting with the will, becomes the power to work. Christ's resurrection gives purpose to human existence on earth, wakening our enthusiasm for the experiences of living and hallowing our will to work in this world in which we live, move and have our being.

The festivals of the winter are naturally celebrated for the most part within doors and those of the spring are related to what is happening outside. Budding branches and flowers just blossoming are the natural decoration for Eastertime. The traditional custom for Easter Sunday is the gift of eggs, which are the symbol of newborn life. The eggs are often coloured, either by being dyed with vegetable dyes or by being painted with designs of pictures. Sometimes greetings and mottoes are written upon them. In many places the style of painting Easter eggs is a part of the old folk art of the district. Few people today know how to produce the intricate old patterns, but it is still good to colour fresh eggs with the best means at hand, rather than to take only imitation ones of chocolate or soap. The living egg is a true symbol of Easter. By an old tradition, early in the morning of Easter Sunday the members of the household should hunt in the garden for coloured eggs, which have been placed there in the night by the Easter hare. Though hares are well known not to lay eggs, this animal is by a very old tradition the guardian and purveyor of these magic coloured ones. As a symbol of fertility, the hare was associated with the forces of the moon. The custom indicates by a picture that the new life on earth is the gift from the powers of the Heavens.

Another symbol of Easter is the butterfly. Starting life as a devouring, crawling caterpillar, this creature passes through a death-like sleep, during which the body is dissolved and reformed in the shape of the brilliant being of the air and the light that flutters among the flowers. The truest picture of the Resurrection in Nature is given in the process by which the caterpillar becomes the butterfly. Its story may be told to children of all ages at Eastertime to help them grasp the thought of death and resurrection. Pictures of butterflies may be used as Easter symbols. Even edible ones can be made, to keep company with the eggs, by using angelica for the bodies and painted rice paper for the wings.

In many churches one large candle is lighted in the night which ends in the dawn of Easter morning and is burnt through the season of the Resurrection to represent the shining of Christ's new risen light. In contrast to the many candles of Christmas time, Easter requires the one very large candle, in a specially-decorated candlestick. Such a usage may well be followed at home, with the same meaning. Once, in ancient times, the fires in the hearths were renewed at this season. The candle flame may remind us of the renewing of the heart's fire within.

Ascension and Whitsuntide

Ascension and Whitsuntide are the seasons of flowers. The trees and plants that come into blossom are the best symbols of what is represented in the festivals. A tree or bush in bloom has made its own ascension, showing as at no other season the heavenly nature of its being. The flowers reach up to the light of the sun and reflect it in their colours. When the petals have dropped and the fruit begins to form, the tree or the bush seems to drop back into its earth-born state. At Whitsuntide, we may see in the open cups of the blossoms, filled with sunlight, the picture for the human hearts that open themselves to be filled full with the light of the Spirit.

At Ascension our attention is directed to the Heavens above, and our imagination reaches out to the worlds of the stars, moon and sun, from which the light-giving, warming, enlivening influences stream down to us. The clouds become for our feeling the threshold between Heaven and earth, the veil that is sometimes thick and dark, at others white and almost transparent. This festival is best celebrated in contemplation of the growing flowers, the moving clouds and the ordered stars. Whitsuntide brings our thoughts back from the heights and widths of the universe into the inner place of the human heart. The fire of the Holy Spirit has descended from above, to burn within the shrine of our souls. Turning within, we seek its light.

Looking to our fellow human beings, we find the flames burning also within them. The spiritual community of Christians, the church, was founded at Whitsuntide in the power of the Holy Spirit. It would be a suitable custom to keep the Easter candle until Whitsun and then give to all the people at hand small candles, which everyone would light for themselves at the flame of the big one. Whatever is undertaken at this festival should lead to an experience of community among human souls who greet the Spirit's flame in each other.

St John's tide

At midsummer is the festival of St John. The usages that have been connected with it in the past belong out of doors, in contrast to those of Christmas. Stress has always been laid on the night, which is the shortest of the year. All the beings living in the elements, that enliven the plants and consort with the animals, are said to be especially active just then. Human beings have to go out into the night and show their activity in the world which they share with other beings and creatures of many kinds. Their sign is the fire lighted on a hilltop at midnight. The flames leap up to greet the twinkling lights of the stars, to proclaim that huma beings are not swallowed up in the darkness, nor overwhelmed in the busy activity of the nature-beings, because an inner spiritual fire burns within them. Dancing and singing should take place through the night hours round the fire, and as it burns lower, those present should jump through the flames. Fire has a purifying force and by passing through the flames the human beings express their desire to be purified of all that which binds them too closely to material existence. By going through the fire without, they seek to burn away what hinders the flame of the Spirit within. Though the custom of lighting midsummer fires is an old one, it can be repeated today with new meaning, when this festival is associated with the Christian figure of St John the Baptist, who kindled the fire in the hearts of those who waited to find Christ.

Michaelmas

The festival of Michaelmas, at the end of September, comes at the time of harvest. Among the old Celtic people special loaves of bread were baked from corn of all the kinds that had been grown that year. So today we may at Michaelmas gather samples of corn, fruit and flowers to celebrate the harvest and bring to mind our gratitude for all that nourishes our life. This alone will not, however, be a true celebration of Michaelmas, for the part of the human being is not sufficiently expressed. An old custom requires that out of the stalks of the corn-straw five-pointed stars should be made. Such a star is a symbol for the human being who, when he stands on the ground with arms and legs outstretched and head raised, is such a five-pointed being. Other customs, which describe the human part in Michaelmas, will have to be discovered in practice as this festival becomes more recognised and honoured in the future. As dancing and music belong to the celebration of summer festivals, so does drama, particularly of the historical kind, to Michaelmas. The great, heroic events of the past may be described in dramatic form, to fire courage and a sense of purpose for the future. At one time, processions round the graveyards were made at this season in honour of the dead. Today the custom may be transformed by letting the deeds of those who went before live in our remembrance to inspire the tasks of the future.

Old customs may be revived in a new sense. New customs may be discovered when people begin to celebrate the festivals within the setting of daily life at home. Only a few simple suggestions have been made here, which have already proved their value in practice.

In such a fashion the spiritual experience of the Christian festivals may cast a bright reflection over the routine of ordinary affairs to enliven it. In our highly civilised urban existence of today, we can come near to ignoring the year's cycle of seasons if we wish, but by so doing we allow all our days and weeks to turn a dull grey. The festivals can bring high and holy days that shine brightly among the work days, if we make room for them in the midst of the daily round. Then they will brighten our lives and enliven our hearts with the touch of their magic.

EPILOGUE

The changing seasons of the year are the reminder that our existence on earth is embedded in the life of the whole star-filled universe. They remind us also, though far less obviously, that the fabric of our life is woven and maintained by the activity of invisible beings who are as much creatures of the universe as are human beings. Today our usual conception of what in reality exists in the world is very limited. Our experiences and our deeper feelings continually warn us of what is beyond our conceptions but we rarely include them in our ways of thinking. Yet we need above everything today to find ideas that will give us the means of knowing more about the greater realities which are present with us, though hidden from our usual understanding. We see, for instance, that the seasons are brought about by the changing relation between the sun and the earth, that they reflect below what happens in the realm above. Our feeling tells us that such a life-giving rhythm must proceed from the activity of living, powerful beings who have their rightful place in the universe. Seeing what is done, we should be logical enough to ask: by whom is all this done?

Until recent times, a treasure of knowledge about the hierarchies of heavenly beings was cherished by generations of Christian thinkers. For a long while, their doctrines have not been the common thinking in churches, but in the early Christian centuries they were so widely known that, for instance, in the epistles of St Paul they are taken for granted. Much of the old doctrine is forgotten today and the Pauline writings have in consequence become very difficult to read aright. Ways of thinking change from age to age. Were more books concerning the old teaching about the hierarchies available, the form of thought would hinder us from grasping their meaning with our minds today. Another source of understanding in this matter has, however, been opened in modern times through the work of Rudolf Steiner. He brought many ideas about the nature of the world and of Man into modern thinking. The facts which he described have often been known before, in earlier ages, but in a very different form of consciousness from ours today. Only now, largely through his work, have they become available to everyone who is interested in such ideas and anxious to think them for himself. Ideas may be thought for the first time, in such a form, by a great spiritual pioneer like Rudolf Steiner, but they can be thought and tested for their truth by anyone who will take them up actively into his own mind.

We know well from appearance the year's round of seasons and festivals, because it is part of our ordinary human life. Yet a deeper reality lies behind, to which we can only penetrate with the help of ideas about the existence of spiritual beings belonging to the company of Heaven. The seasons come and go, but who guides their course, who inspires the mood of soul that breathes through the particular atmosphere we feel with each in turn? Four great spiritual guardians watch over a part of the year, each following the other in order. They are archangels, Gabriel, Raphael, Uriel and Michael. The season of the year before and after Christmas is under the care of Gabriel. That around and following Easter has Raphael for guardian. Midsummer, both before and after, belongs to Uriel. The late summer and autumn is the season, even in popular language, of Michael.

Gabriel is the archangel of the Annunciation, he of whom we read in the Gospel of St Luke that he was sent by the Lord to tell Mary that she would bear the child who would bring salvation. By old tradition, his emblem is the white lily. The forces which he wields are connected with the mysteries of birth, of Spirit descending into the sphere of matter. His influence sends into our hearts the spiritual experience that is characteristic of midwinter and the Christmas festivals. When we follow his inspiration, we look back in thought to the origin of our being in the Divine World. Each soul has lived before birth in the company of the beings of God and has journeyed through the kingdoms of the stars. He has been carried down from the heights of the world to the depths of earth by angelic hands. He has been sent into earthly life with a store of strength and manifold capacities of soul and body bestowed upon him by his heavenly guardians. The birth of each human being recalls the creation of Man at the beginning of time by the hand of God. All that is within us, all that is around us in the created world, has come forth from the realms of Spirit. The Divine World underlies all things and is the source of all life. The archangel of the winter brings before our souls the remembrance of our origin, in reverence for that which comes from God. If we follow his influence weaving in the true mood of wintertime, he leads us to behold the mystery of the Christmas festival, the birth into earth of that which comes from the heights of the Heavens.

Raphael is the archangel of healing. He looks with compassion upon the sick state into which human beings have fallen through the influence of the powers of evil. He is not the only one of the company of Heaven to feel compassion for Mankind. All the divine beings serving the true purposes of God have such feelings towards the children of humanity, when they see how poor they have become compared with the ideal from which they were created. They desire to send healing to these sick and fallen creatures on earth. Raphael is able to gather the forces of divine compassion and direct them towards human souls. He wields the spiritual powers of healing in his office of archangel. By old tradition his symbol is the staff of the healer. In springtime, when the beauties of Nature are renewed, human beings feel how much they need new life in themselves, which they cannot receive from the world around. Raphael calls in this season the souls of those who will listen to his influence, to perceive the presence of the healing Spirit within. He becomes our inner guide into the mystery of Easter, Ascension and Whitsuntide. Those who can hear the thoughts inspired by him learn year by year to penetrate more deeply into the understanding of Christ's deed of death and life, which He performed on earth to save humans from losing their humanity through the sickness of sin and the infection of death. Raphael teaches our souls to see the way of salvation by which we may be healed by the Spirit.

Uriel is the archangel who calls to us from the world-heights at the season of midsummer. All creatures of the kingdoms of Nature are looking upward at this time, sending the forces of their being up to meet the world's light in the Heavens. That which is in the state of matter strives towards the Spirit. Unknown though this may be to all but the deepest feelings of our hearts, a harvesting of what is good and bad in the souls of men and women takes place at this season under the eyes of the angels. Uriel cares for the force of conscience in our inner being, warning us to strengthen our sense of right and wrong. He requires us to look into our deeds, to review not only that which belongs to our personal affairs but to that part which we bear in the history of our time within the whole evolution of Mankind. We should consider the fruits of our thinking and doing as they appear to the stern but just archangel, who looks down on our life and calls us to awaken and listen to the inner voice of our conscience. When the sun has reached his zenith in the sky, and Nature the time of abundant blossom and fruit, human beings are summoned by the call of Uriel to look within and renew the strength of their moral nature.

Michael is the archangel who guides us through the time when the life of Nature dies down and the sun's light declines. The shadow of death falls over the earth and human souls should turn to find their strength from the Spirit within. By old tradition, he is the fighting archangel, who withstands the dragon, the power of Evil. He sends us forces of heart to strengthen our courage to face Evil and hold our own. He wields the power of pure, spirit-devoted will that is offered in service to Christ, before whose mystery he stands guard. His emblem of old was the sword or spear, accompanied by the scales of justice. As Gabriel guides souls on their way down into birth, so Michael accompanies them on the path towards death. In modern times, a side of his nature has come to the fore that was earlier less clearly known. He rouses and cherishes in human beings the forces of thinking capable of comprehending the deed of Christ. He would inspire us to find an understanding faith which, beginning in thought, can send inspiration into the will and make us into active, thinking followers of Him whom he serves. He stands before our souls and calls us with a powerful gesture to follow his guidance into the search for true Christianity.

Behind the outer round of winter, spring, summer and autumn, the inner meetings take place with Gabriel, Raphael, Uriel and Michael. Each offers to people his especial blessing within his portion of the seasons. The regent over the whole circle of the year, because, as so often has been described in these pages, He has united His life with that of the earth, is Christ Himself. He is revealed to us in the festivals, from one aspect and then from another, until He has shown us Himself in the whole vision that is too great to be seen at once. Each of the four archangels stands in His service as guardian before one part of the revelation, rousing in us the forces of soul which will best fit us to partake therein.

He who came from the heights of the universe to bring salvation to human souls lives now in Spirit among us in the world of earth. He is here and He speaks to us through each of the festivals that come again and again with the changing seasons. "As long as I am in the world, I am the light of the world": so He spoke of Himself. His light shines upon the ways of our earth existence, day by day, year by year, until the world's end.

The Spirit Within Us

Evelyn Capel

Many people today find themselves in situations with which they cannot cope. How often do we have to make decisions for which we feel we don't have enough wisdom? How often do we have overwhelming experiences? How often do we feel, if only I could be wiser or more courageous to help me deal with the events, the people, the problems, and the decisions that face me?

Evelyn Capel argues that each one of us has a source of strength within ourselves: the spirit of Christ. By developing an active inner life, the spirit within us can be found and brought into our consciousness.

Doing this requires thought and care, and in this inspiring book Capel offers practical and compassionate advice. She considers the rhythm of the day, as well as issues of concentration and meditation, to help the reader cultivate their inner life.

www.florisbooks.co.uk